UPLAND GAME BIRDS

THE HUNTING & FISHING LIBRARY®

By Dick Sternberg

DICK STERNBERG has hunted most kinds of upland game birds found in North America, but he's particularly fond of chasing ringnecks with his black lab "Nicky."

CY DECOSSE INCORPORATED

 A COWLES MAGAZINES COMPANY

Chairman/CEO: Bruce Barnet
Chairman Emeritus: Cy DeCosse
President/COO: Nino Tarantino
Executive V.P./Editor-in-Chief: William B. Jones

UPLAND GAME BIRDS

Author and Project Director: Dick Sternberg
Book Development Leaders: Steve Hauge, Mike Hehner
Technical Advisor: Ron Spomer
Executive Editor: Don Oster
Editor: Janice Cauley
Project Managers: Denise Bornhausen, John van Vliet
Senior Art Directors: Dave Schelitzche, Brad Springer
Art Directors: Kathlynn Henthorne, John Hermanson, Geoffrey Kinsey
Researchers: Steve Hauge, Mike Hehner, Dave Maas, Jim Moynagh
V. P. Development Planning and Production: Jim Bindas
Creative Photo Coordinator: Cathleen Shannon
Director of Photography: Mike Parker
Studio Manager: Marcia Chambers
Principal Photographers: William Lindner, Mike Hehner
Staff Photographer: Mark Macemon
Contributing Photographers: Grady Allen, Steve Bentsen, Mike Blair, Denver Bryan, Gary W. Carter, George Conrad/Sporting Clays Magazine, Daniel J. Cox, Mike & Dena Creel, Rob Curtis/Vireo, Larry R. Ditto, Jeanne Drake, Gary William Griffen, David Kenyon, Lon E. Lauber, H. Lea Lawrence, Tim Leary, Jim Levy/The Wildside, Steve Maas, Bill Marchel, Wyman Meinzer, William H. Mullins, Alan G. Nelson/Dembinsky Photo Associates, Aaron Fraser Pass, John E. Phillips, Leonard Lee Rue III, Tony Sailer/The Brainerd Daily Dispatch, Nick Sisley, Dale C. Spartas, Ron Spomer, Judith E. Strom, Ron Winch, Gary R. Zahm, Dale & Marian Zimmerman/Vireo, Jim Zumbo
Photo Assistants: Pat Connelly, Steve Hauge, Mike Hehner, Dave Maas, Jim Moynagh, John van Vliet
Senior Publishing Production Manager: Laurie Gilbert
Senior Desktop Publishing Specialist: Joe Fahey
Production Staff: Willis Alexander, Amy Berndt, Mike Schauer, Nik Wogstad
Illustrators: Thomas Boll, Dave Schelitzche

Contributing Manufacturers: The Boyt Co.; Browning Arms Co. – Paul Thompson; Cabela's – Tony Dolle; The C. C. Filson Co. – Steve Matson; Federal Cartridge Co. – Bill Stevens; Irish Setter Boots – John DePalma; Normark Corp. – Shaun Kuffel; The Orvis Co. – Tim Joseph, Tom Rosenbauer

Contributing Individuals and Agencies: Tom Andersen; Arizona Game and Fish Dept. – Ron Engle-Wilson; Arnold Design – Tom Ostrom; Damon Bartolo; Bert Benshoof; Burger Brothers – John Goplin; California Dept. of Fish and Game –

D. Sam Blankenship; Charles E. Carpenter; Dave Carty; Bob Cassell; Pat Connelly; George Conrad; Chris Dorsey; Flood Creek Hunting Preserve – Todd Peterson; Georgia Dept. of Natural Resources – Haven Barnhill, Ron Simpson; Tom & Verna Gertgen; Gayle & Steve Grossman; Leon Hart; Kevin Haugan; Bob Hirsch; Jim Hooker; Dennis Hunt; Idaho Dept. of Fish and Game – Darryl Meintes; Indian Hills Resort – Byron, Kelly Jo & Tolly Holtan; J. Rex & Associates – Jim Rex; Rob Johnstone; Kansas Dept. of Wildlife and Parks – Kevin Church; Quentin Kramer; Lac Qui Parle Hunting Camp – Steve Baldwin, Terry Norby; Little Moran Hunting Club; Martin/Williams Agency – Mike Bruner; Mike Murphy & Sons – Jim Greenwood; Minnesota Horse & Hunt Club – Dick Rice; Minnesota Valley Taxidermy – Jack Cudd, Terry Mergens; Moon Valley Range – Hans Madsen; Nevada Dept. of Wildlife – Mike Cox; North Dakota Tourism – Dawn Charging, Kevin Cramer, Jim Fuglie; Olin-Winchester – Dave Price; John Oliver; Shawn Perich; Pheasants Forever – Jay Johnson; Rum River Pheasant Club – Rick Johnson; John Schneider; Bob Schranck; Shamrock Shooting Preserve – Pat Finnegan; Sport Sales Inc. – Red Reichert; State Line Resort – Diana & Ken Moser; Dr. Tom Tacha; Texas Parks and Wildlife Dept. – Ron George; Thorne Brothers; Jim Werre; Dale Westerberg; Wildlife Research Center – Clait E. Braun; Dee Wilkerson; Wing & Shot Magazine – Roger Sparks; Mike Woodside; Wyoming Fish and Game Dept. – Harry Harju; Keith Zemke

Printing: R. R. Donnelley & Sons Co. (0695)

Copyright © 1995 by Cy DeCosse Incorporated
5900 Green Oak Drive
Minnetonka, Minnesota 55343
1-800-328-3895

Library of Congress
Cataloging-in-Publication Data

Sternberg, Dick.
Upland game birds / by Dick Sternberg.
p. cm. – (The Hunting & fishing library)
Includes index.
ISBN 0-86573-042-3
1. Upland game bird shooting. I. Title. II. Series.
SK323.S75 1995   95-4066
799.2'42—dc20

Also available from the publisher:

The Art of Freshwater Fishing, Cleaning & Cooking Fish, Fishing With Live Bait, Largemouth Bass, Panfish, The Art of Hunting, Fishing With Artificial Lures, Walleye, Smallmouth Bass, Dressing & Cooking Wild Game, Freshwater Gamefish of North America, Trout, Secrets of the Fishing Pros, Fishing Rivers & Streams, Fishing Tips & Tricks, Fishing Natural Lakes, White-tailed Deer, Northern Pike & Muskie, America's Favorite Fish Recipes, Fishing Man-made Lakes, The Art of Fly Tying, America's Favorite Wild Game Recipes, Advanced Bass Fishing

Contents

Introduction

Whether it's a covey of bobwhites exploding from a bush, or a big ringneck busting out of a clump of slough grass, the excitement of the flush explains why upland bird hunting gets in your blood.

Unlike many other types of hunting that require traveling long distances or having connections in order to find a productive spot, upland bird hunting is easily accessible to most anyone. With the variety of birds available, and the wide distribution of many, chances are you can hunt for some kind of upland bird within a short drive of your home.

This book is intended to acquaint you with every important type of upland bird hunting done in North America. You'll learn how to hunt pheasants, six kinds of quail, two kinds of partridge and six kinds of grouse, plus doves, woodcock and more. Besides information about the bird, itself, we'll show you the habitat in which it lives and the most productive hunting techniques.

To collect the latest and best hunting information for each kind of bird, our staff traveled to dozens of diverse bird-hunting areas across the country, spent time afield with local experts and photographed their most productive hunting techniques, along with their favorite tips and tricks for finding and outwitting their feathered quarry.

Before you can hunt birds successfully, you'll need the right equipment. We'll show you how to select the right shotgun for each type of hunting, how to determine if your gun fits properly and what you can do to correct the problem if it doesn't. You'll also find information on choosing the right shotgun shells and checking your gun's "pattern" for proper shot distribution.

Wingshooting is an art, and many hunters find that it takes years to become proficient at it. Our section on shooting techniques will help you shorten that time considerably. After acquainting you with the three most common wingshooting techniques, we give you some excellent tips that are sure to improve your shooting eye.

The quickest way to ruin a good bird hunt is to wear the wrong clothing. Besides showing you the latest in coats, vests, caps, gloves, boots, socks and even shooting glasses, we explain how to dress for different types of terrain and weather conditions.

Dogs are a vital part of most upland bird hunts, and many hunters would not even consider going afield without one. This book won't give you all the information you need on selecting, training and caring for a hunting dog, but it does provide a short primer, along with a pictorial guide to the most popular pointing and flushing/retrieving breeds.

It's not only the thrill of the flush that gives upland bird hunting its near-universal appeal. It's also the challenge of wingshooting and the companionship of a favorite bird dog – not to speak of the great exercise you get from tromping after pheasants in a cattail swamp or chasing chukars up a mountainside. Reading this book will help you perfect your bird-hunting techniques and make the sport even more enjoyable.

Equipment & Dogs

HINGE ACTION. The action opens when you push a lever or button at the rear of the receiver, allowing you to manually insert the shells. After firing, you break the

Shotguns

You can pay as much for a fine, intricately engraved shotgun as you would a luxury car, but you'll bag just as many birds with an inexpensive gun. When making your selection, it's important to consider action, gauge, chamber length, barrel length and choke.

ACTION. Most upland bird hunters use one of these three actions:

• Hinge. A hinge, or break, action is used in single-shots and double-barrels. Considered the classic upland bird guns, double-barrels are reliable, safe and stylish, but quite expensive. They come in side-by-side and over-and-under models.

Some hunters prefer side-by-sides because of the wider sighting plane, but if you're accustomed to shooting a rifle, you'll feel more comfortable with an over-and-under.

action again. If your gun has *ejectors*, the spent hulls will pop out automatically; otherwise, you must remove them yourself.

Although double-barrels give you only two shots, you have the option of selecting different chokes for each barrel. Most double-barrels have a single trigger, although some have a separate one for each barrel. The firing order of the barrels may be predetermined, or you may be able to change the order by pushing a lever on the receiver.

• Semi-automatic. Many shooters feel their concentration is better with a semi-automatic shotgun than with a pump, because no arm movement is needed and there is considerably less recoil. But semi-automatics are more likely to jam or otherwise malfunction, because of the complex internal mechanism. Jamming is most likely under cold or dusty conditions, especially if the gun is dirty.

Semi-automatics come in gas- or recoil-operated models. Recoil-operated guns are more reliable, but tend to "kick" more. Gas-operated guns work better for shooting light loads.

• Pump. Economical and reliable, pumps enable you to shoot just as rapidly as you would with a semi-automatic, with much less chance of jamming.

SEMI-AUTOMATIC ACTION. A semi-automatic fires one shell, ejects it and chambers another with each pull of the trigger. Most semi-automatics hold 5 shells, although a few hold up to 7.

PUMP-ACTION. A pump ejects the spent shell and chambers another one each time you slide the fore-end back and forth. The majority of pump-action shotguns hold 5 shells.

Bores used in upland bird hunting (actual size)

GAUGE. The smaller the gauge number, the larger the bore diameter. Upland bird guns range from 12 to 28 gauge, with 12s and 20s being the most popular. Although the .410 (measured in inches rather than gauge) is often billed as a good gun for beginners, we do not recommend it; the small pattern and low pellet count of the ammunition result in a high crippling rate.

The 12-gauge is the most versatile bore for upland bird hunting. With heavy loads, it's adequate for pheasants and other large birds. With light loads, it can be used for the smallest quail. A 12-gauge generally gives you higher muzzle velocity, a denser shot pattern and more downrange energy than a 20, but it is heavier and less maneuverable, with greater recoil.

The 16-gauge, once considered a good compromise, has lost popularity in recent years, probably because of the increasing use and excellent performance of 3-inch magnum 20-gauge shells.

Some quail, grouse and woodcock hunters swear by the 28-gauge, because of its maneuverability, but it is not a good choice for big birds. Both 16- and 28-gauge shells are difficult to find in many areas.

CHAMBER LENGTH. Many shotguns come in either standard or magnum models. Standard chambers take 2¾-inch shells; magnums, 3- or 3½-inch, depending on the gauge. The proper shell length is usually stamped on the barrel. Standard chambers are adequate for most upland bird hunting, but magnums give you a little extra range, an advantage when the birds are flushing wild. Be sure you know what type of shell your gun can handle; the wrong one could cause a chamber explosion that results in serious injury.

BARREL LENGTH. A longer barrel gives you more accuracy, because the heavier weight ensures a better follow-through. The extra length also means slightly higher shot velocity, which extends your effective shooting range a bit. But a long barrel is not practical for most types of upland bird hunting, because it's too cumbersome in heavy cover. With the exception of pass-shooting, or late-season hunting for spooky birds, there's no need for a barrel longer than 28 inches and, usually, no more than 26. The trend is toward even shorter barrels – 24 or 25 inches. Not only are short barrels easier to maneuver in cover, they make a gun lighter and quicker to shoulder.

A ventilated rib makes a good sighting plane and helps cool the barrel quickly, an advantage for dove hunting or any other rapid-fire shooting.

CHOKE. The amount of constriction, or choke, at the end of the barrel affects the diameter and density of your shot pattern (below). Common chokes, from widest (most open) to narrowest (tightest), include: cylinder, skeet, improved-cylinder, modified, improved-modified and full. Open chokes are best for close-range shooting; tight chokes, long-range. The improved-cylinder is a good all-around choice.

Many modern shotguns have interchangeable screw-in choke tubes that enable you to quickly change chokes to suit the type of hunting. A gunsmith can also install screw-in chokes in older guns.

Choke vs. Effective Shooting Range

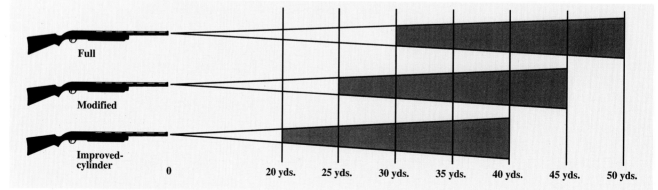

SELECT your choke based on the distance at which you'll be doing most of your shooting. With a modified choke, for instance, the pattern is effective out to 45 yards, but, below 25 yards, it would be too small and dense. Your chances of hitting a bird would be low, and, if you did hit it, you would damage too much meat.

CHECK length of pull by shouldering the gun and sighting as you normally would. There should be a space of approximately 2 to 3 inches between the base of your thumb and the tip of your nose. The inset photo shows you how to measure length of pull, drop at heel and drop at comb.

Shotgun Fit

To shoot comfortably and accurately, you must have a shotgun that fits properly. Following are the important elements of proper fit:

Length of pull is the distance from the butt of the stock to the trigger. The standard measurement is 14¼ inches. You can check the length of pull as shown above.

If the stock is too long, you won't be able to shoulder the gun without the butt catching on your cloth-ing. The solution is to have a gunsmith shorten the stock. If the stock is too short, your cheek will rest too far forward on the comb and the base of your thumb may jam against your nose, making it difficult to sight properly. You can lengthen the stock by adding a recoil pad.

Drop at comb and *drop at heel* also affect your ability to sight properly. Drop at comb is the distance from the plane of the barrel to the top of the comb; drop at heel, the distance from the plane to the top of the heel, or butt. Unless these measurements are correct, your eyes will not line up properly with the plane of the barrel, so you will not shoot accurately.

The standard measurement for drop at comb is 1½ inches; drop at heel, 2½ inches. These measurements should be a little less for a short person, a little more for a tall one.

If you're not sure if your shotgun fits properly, have it checked at a gun shop. They may be able to modify the stock or custom-make one for you.

Shotgun Shells

When selecting shotgun shells, consider load (amount of powder and shot) and shot size. Field loads, also known as dove-and-quail or game loads, have the least powder and shot, and the shot is softer than in most other loads. As a result, it deforms easily, meaning more "flyers," pellets that sail too far from the center of the pattern. Standard loads, also called high-power loads, have more powder and shot; magnum loads, more yet.

Standard loads are a good all-around choice for upland bird hunting. Field loads are adequate for small- to medium-size birds, particularly at close ranges, and are much less expensive. Magnums give you a denser long-range pattern, which is often needed in late-season hunting.

Most manufacturers offer an additional line of high-grade shells. This ammunition has plated lead shot, which, when surrounded by plastic buffering material, reduces shot deformation, resulting in a more even pattern with fewer flyers.

SHOT SHELL PARTS include:
(1) hull, the outer shell, usually made of plastic or paper, with a metal base; (2) shot, round lead or steel pellets; (3) powder, which is ignited by (4) primer when firing pin strikes it; (5) wad, a plastic or fiber divider that separates powder and shot.

Shot size depends on the size of the bird and the distance at which you do most of your shooting. Upland bird hunters use shot from sizes 4 to 9 (below). For small targets, like quail, use shot from size 7½ to 9. It gives you a dense pattern, yet has enough energy for clean kills.

Larger shot would give you a looser pattern, possibly with holes large enough for small birds to fly through. And if the shot connects, it would damage too much meat. There is seldom a need for shot larger than size 6, although some late-season hunters use 4s to down big birds at long range.

State or federal regulations sometimes require steel shot for upland birds when you're hunting in a waterfowl-production area or some other spot where there is a chance that waterfowl would ingest the spent pellets. Because steel is lighter, you'll need shot two sizes larger than you would if using lead. Size 4 steel, for instance, is a substitute for size 6 lead.

Average Pellet Count *(lead shot)*

SHOT SIZES	WEIGHT OF SHOT IN OUNCES								
	¾	⅞	1	1⅛	1¼	1⅜	1½	1⅝	1⅞
9	439	512	585	658	731	804	877	951	1097
8½	373	435	497	559	621	683	745	808	932
8	307	359	410	461	512	564	615	666	769
7½	262	306	350	394	437	481	525	569	656
6	169	197	225	253	281	309	337	366	422
5	127	149	170	191	212	234	255	276	319
4	101	118	135	152	169	186	202	219	253

Recommended Shot Sizes

GAME	SHOT SIZES
Pheasants, Prairie Chicken Sharp-tailed & Sage Grouse	4, 5, 6, 7½
Gray & Chukar Partridge Ruffed, Spruce & Blue Grouse	6, 7½, 8
Doves, Pigeons & Woodcock	7½, 8
Mountain & Gambel's Quail	6, 7½, 8
Bobwhite, Scaled, Mearn's & California Quail	7½, 8, 9
Ptarmigan	7½

How to Pattern a Shotgun

Not all shotguns shoot alike, so even if you select the right choke and the proper shell, you'll still have to test-shoot your gun and examine the shot distribution on a target. This procedure is called *patterning*.

Hang a wrapping-paper target in a safe spot, stand 40 yards away and fire at a bull's-eye. Check the target; the bull's-eye should be in the center of the densest part of the pattern. If it isn't, there may be a problem with your gun or the ammunition you're using.

Assuming the pattern is centered over the bull's-eye, draw a 30-inch circle and calculate the percentage of pellets inside it as described at right. Then, compare this percentage with the standard figures given in the bar graph below. With an improved-cylinder choke, for instance, the figure should be 40 to 45 percent.

If you have a screw-in choke system, experiment with different choke tubes to achieve the desired pattern. You can also experiment with different types of shells. If you still can't achieve the desired pattern, consult a gun shop. If the choke is too tight, they can bore it out. If it's too loose, they can add a screw-in choke.

When you examine your pattern, make sure there are no big holes (gaps in the pattern) in it. Holes may result from an overly loose choke, or an overly tight one, which causes excessive pellet deformation. Too many holes cause crippling and may allow birds to fly through your pattern. It's a good idea to shoot at several targets for dependable patterning results.

DRAW a 30-inch circle around the center of the densest part of your pattern. Count the number of pellets inside the circle, divide by the number of pellets in the load and multiply this number by 100. This figure is the percentage of shot in a 30-inch circle at 40 yards.

Shot Density vs. Choke

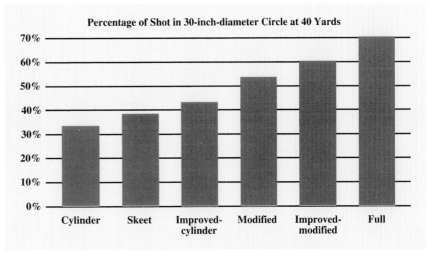

Percentage of Shot in 30-inch-diameter Circle at 40 Yards

Cylinder — Skeet — Improved-cylinder — Modified — Improved-modified — Full

PROPER SHOOTING FORM (right-handed). Stand with left foot slightly forward, keeping feet about shoulder-width apart and pointed at a 45-degree angle to the target. Bend knees slightly, and lean forward a little at the waist.

Shooting Techniques

Rarely does a novice hunter pick up a shotgun and immediately start downing birds. Even if you understand basic shotgunning principles and have the proper shooting form (above), it takes a good deal of practice to get the feel of quickly shouldering the gun and swinging it smoothly, and to become accustomed to the recoil.

When you're walking, carry the gun in a manner that will allow you to bring it up rapidly. If you carry it over your shoulder, for instance, you'll have to bring the gun down and reposition your hands before you can shoot. By that time, the bird may be out of range. It would be better to carry the gun across your body, with your trigger hand beneath the front of the stock and your other hand beneath the fore-end. This way, you can shoulder the gun in a fraction of a second.

If your gun fits properly (p. 11), you should be able to bring it to your shoulder without it catching on your clothing. With the butt snugged up against your shoulder, your cheek should rest comfortably on the side of the comb. With both eyes open, sight straight down the barrel with your dominant eye, which, for most right-handed shooters, is the right eye. If you are right-handed, but your left eye is dominant, try squinting your left eye while sighting with your right.

The majority of hunters, regardless of experience level, tend to shoot behind crossing birds and under rising birds. They fail to realize that in the fraction of a second from the time they pull the trigger to the time the shot arrives where they were aiming, the target has moved several feet.

Simply exaggerating your lead is not necessarily the answer. To shoot effectively under a variety of conditions, you must learn these shooting techniques:

Basic Wing-shooting Techniques

SNAP-SHOOTING. This technique is recommended for close-range shooting in thick cover, when you don't have much time to aim. When a bird explodes from dense brush, for instance, quickly point your barrel at the spot where you think the bird will be when the shot arrives, and pull the trigger.

SWING-THROUGH. The most widely used technique in upland bird hunting, the swing-through method is ideal for midrange crossing shots where cover density is not a consideration. By starting with the barrel pointing behind the bird and swinging it smoothly ahead until it's just past the bird before pulling the trigger, you automatically attain the proper lead. But even the swing-through technique won't stop you from shooting behind the bird unless you complete the swing with a smooth follow-through. The tendency is to swing ahead of the bird, then stop swinging when you shoot. Frequent practice is the only way to train yourself to follow through.

SUSTAINED LEAD. Used mainly for pass-shooting at high-flying birds, such as doves and pigeons, this method involves pointing the barrel well ahead of the target, swinging to maintain a consistent lead as the target moves, then pulling the trigger while continuing to maintain the lead. Once you learn to properly estimate leads at different ranges and angles, this technique gives you better long-range accuracy than the swing-through technique.

SHOOT at clay targets thrown with a hand trap to hone your wing-shooting skills. Have the thrower try to dupli-cate problematical shooting situations, such as crossing shots and over-the-head shots.

JOIN a skeet- or trap-shooting league, which enables you to practice a variety of shooting angles and distances, while offering some friendly competition.

WORK with a professional instructor to identify problems in your shooting technique. A good instructor can instantly spot flaws that would be nearly impossible to detect on your own.

PRACTICE shooting at a sporting clays course. While walking through a wooded course, you'll shoot at clay targets that simulate a wide variety of real wing-shooting situations.

Cleaning, Lubrication and Maintenance Tips

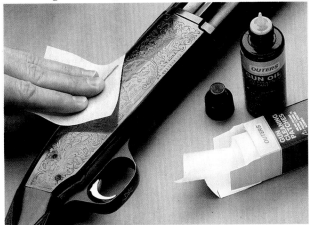

RUB your gun's entire surface with a light coat of gun oil after each use. Even if the gun appears dry, imperceptible amounts of moisture can cause rust spots and pitting.

CLEAN the gas ports in a gas-operated semi-automatic with a pipe cleaner. If the ports clog up with powder residue, there won't be enough pressure to eject the empties.

ADD a desiccant pack to your guncase and zip it up for long-term storage. The desiccant absorbs moisture, preventing rust from developing.

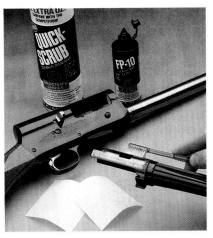

BRUSH the top of the barrel and the roof of the receiver of a recoil-operated gun to remove residue, which prevents shell ejection. Oil lightly.

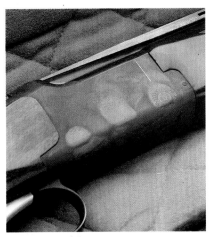

AVOID keeping your gun in a cold car. Condensation forms as soon as you bring the gun inside, causing corrosion of the metal.

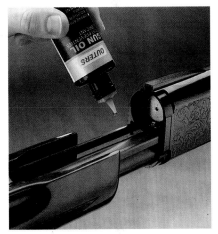

LUBRICATE each receiver track of a pump or semi-automatic with light gun oil so the action works more freely.

SPRAY gun scrub into the open action to remove dirt and residue. Use short blasts, continuing until the solvent runs clean.

APPLY a light coat of oil to the magazine tube of a semi-automatic, after cleaning it with gun scrub. This ensures enough recoil to eject the empties.

TYPICAL ATTIRE for upland bird hunting includes a hunting vest worn over a light jacket or shirt, chaps, leather boots, blaze-orange cap, thin-leather shooting gloves and shooting glasses.

Clothing for Upland Bird Hunting

Upland bird hunters need different types of clothing for different weather conditions and types of terrain. Following are some guidelines for selecting bird-hunting clothes and accessories:

COATS AND VESTS. Beginners often make the mistake of buying a hunting coat that's too heavy, so they're sweating after a few minutes of walking, even in below-freezing weather. A heavy coat also restricts arm movement, making it difficult to shoot accurately.

For most bird hunting, all you need is a shell vest or light hunting jacket. Vests, which come in "skeleton" models (left) and traditional models (right), are very popular, because they're comfortable and allow free arm movement.

A hunting jacket should be large enough so you can wear a heavy shirt or sweater under it in cold weather. A good jacket or vest has a hard-enough finish that it won't catch burrs, yet is flexible enough that it doesn't restrict your movement. It should have a game bag in the rear, preferably with a liner that won't soak up blood, and shell holders in the pockets or on the front. Look for pockets with reinforced corners that won't tear out.

The upper portion of your coat or vest should have some blaze orange so other hunters can see you in high or dense cover, such as tall grass. Although some hunters shy away from blaze orange because they believe it makes them too visible to the birds, the fact is that most birds see or hear you, or detect ground vibrations, long before you're within shooting range.

Most bird hunters are reluctant to venture out in rainy weather, because even a light mist or snow will soak an ordinary hunting coat. And most rain gear is of little use, because brushy or thorny cover would soon shred it. The best solution is to choose a Gore-Tex® coat or one with an oiled or waxed outer shell.

POPULAR hunting boots include (1) insulated leather-Cordura® boots, (2) lightweight leather-Cordura hiking boots, (3) leather boots, (4) rubber-leather packs, (5) rubber boots and (6) leather snake boots.

PANTS. Like a good hunting coat, hunting pants should be burrproof, yet flexible. For hunting in dense brush or thorny cover, choose heavy Cordura pants (left) or pants with canvas facing; for lighter brush, nylon-faced pants (right). Lightweight cotton pants (middle) work well for warm-weather hunting in light cover. For hunting in wet grass, consider buying oiled, waxed or Gore-Tex pants. Or, buy chaps that can be worn over any pants (opposite). When hunting snake country in warm weather, wear snakeproof leggings made from heavy canvas or Cordura, or use snake boots.

BOOTS. Selecting the right boots can be a big problem for upland bird hunters. There is no single style that suits all the conditions you're likely to encounter.

In hot weather, the best choice is an unlined boot made of thin leather, such as kangaroo hide, or a leather-Cordura combination. In cool weather, select a leather or leather-Cordura boot with a layer of good insulation, such as Thinsulate®. In very cold weather, you'll need packs, which have rubber bottoms, leather uppers and felt or Thinsulate liners. If you don't have packs, you can greatly improve the insulating qualities of an ordinary pair of boots by adding felt insoles. Cold-weather boots must be large enough to accommodate heavy socks. Otherwise, they'll restrict your circulation and your feet will feel cold. In snake country, hunters often wear heavy, calf-high, leather or Cordura boots.

If you'll be hunting in muddy fields or wet grass, be sure your boots are waterproof. Some top-quality leather boots are water-resistant, if you keep them treated with silicone or petroleum-based boot dressing. But for total water protection, you'll need rubber boots or boots with a layer of Gore-Tex sandwiched between the shell and liner. Gore-Tex allows your boots to breathe, so perspiration build-up is not as much of a problem as it is with rubber.

An often-overlooked consideration is the type of sole. Rubber, crepe or urethane soles with a shallow tread are the best all-around choice. They're waterproof, flexible and easy to clean, yet give you adequate traction under most conditions.

Lug soles give you better traction in steep, rocky terrain, but they're a poor choice for muddy fields. Mud that collects in the treads makes your feet heavy, and you'll track it into your car or wherever else you go.

Whatever boots you choose, be sure to break them in before the hunting season. If nothing else, wear them around the house once in a while. If you put them on for the first time on opening day, you're virtually assured of winding up with blisters. To keep your boots flexible and water-resistant, treat them frequently with boot dressing.

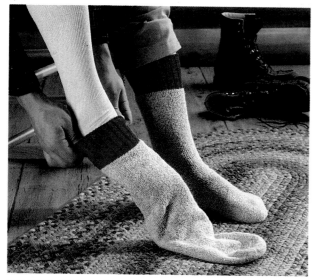

SOCKS. Thin polypropylene socks, worn beneath medium- to heavyweight wool, Thinsulate or polypropylene socks, wick moisture into the heavier outer layer. They keep your feet dryer, warmer and less likely to blister than the heavier socks by themselves. Gore-Tex socks keep your feet dry, even if your boots leak.

GLOVES. Shooting gloves, made of very thin deerskin or cowhide, protect your hands from thorns and briars, yet give you a secure grip and good trigger feel. With cotton or wool gloves, you'll have a hard time getting a secure grip on the fore-end, unless they have a nonslip, rubberized palm. In below-freezing weather, try fingerless gloves made of heavier wool.

SHOOTING GLASSES. A pair of glasses with lenses made of plastic, polycarbonate, shatter-resistant glass or scratch-resistant thermoplastic will protect your eyes from thorns, dust, stray pellets or debris from a chamber explosion. Shooting glasses come with clear or specially tinted lenses. Smoke-colored lenses (top) cut down glare on bright days; yellow lenses (bottom) brighten things up on cloudy days.

Most shooting glasses have flexible-wire temples to hold them on firmly and brow bars (arrow) to prevent sweat from getting into your eyes. Prescription shooting glasses may be available through your optometrist.

HEADWEAR. Most upland bird hunters wear baseball-style caps, because they're comfortable and the visor helps shade their eyes. Choose a light, mesh-backed cap (lower left) for warm-weather hunting; a heavier, foam-lined cap in colder weather. Some hunters wear stocking caps (lower right) or caps with ear flaps, but unless the weather is extremely cold, it's better to keep your ears uncovered; otherwise, you may not hear the birds flush and probably won't see them until it's too late. You can buy a waterproof hat (upper left) for use in rainy weather or a light, wide-brimmed hat (upper right) for hot, sunny weather. Blaze orange is recommended, especially when you're hunting in a group or in tall cover.

CARRY a pack with the following accessories: (1) extra socks, should your feet get wet; (2) vicinity map; (3) potassium pills, to help maintain your electrolyte balance in hot weather; (4) sealable plastic bags to hold dressed birds; (5) matches in a waterproof case; (6) pocket knife with gutting hook, for field-dressing birds; (7) game shears, for cutting up birds; (8) flashlight; (9) compass; (10) canteen. You'll also need (11) a shell box and shells with various shot sizes.

ACCESSORIES. You may not need all of the items shown above, but it's a good idea to keep an accessory pack in your vehicle. It's important to have a pocket knife on a hot day, for instance, because you'll want to field-dress your birds soon after you shoot them. Keep a cooler with ice in your vehicle, and drop off the birds after each leg of your hunt.

FIRST-AID SUPPLIES. Always carry first-aid supplies (right) for yourself and your dog. Your first-aid kit should contain adhesive strips, gauze, adhesive tape and first-aid cream, for dressing blisters and minor cuts from thorns and barbed wire. A snakebite kit with a venom extractor is a must, if you'll be hunting in snake country.

For your dog, carry forceps for removing thorns and cactus spines; wound cream; self-sticking wrap, for protecting bandages; and eyewash. Use the gauze and adhesive tape from your first-aid kit.

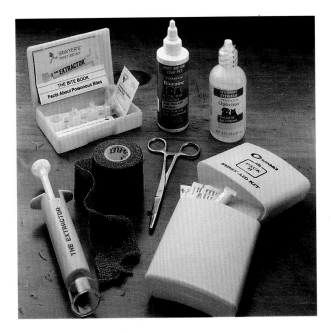

Dogs for Upland Bird Hunting

For many experienced hunters, good dog work is much more important than bagging birds. Seeing a staunch, picture-book point or watching a flusher root a bird out of thick cover is the most satisfying part of the hunt. And the close companionship that develops between hunter and dog adds another dimension to the hunting experience.

A well-trained dog is an indispensable tool for most types of upland bird hunting. Not only will it locate more birds for you, it will greatly boost your odds of recovering the ones you shoot. But a poorly trained dog is worse than no dog at all. It will run too far ahead of the hunters and flush the birds before they get there. If it does find a downed bird, it may chew it to bits.

The best breed depends on the kinds of birds you hunt and where you hunt them. A pointing dog is ideal for pinning down tight-holding birds, like bobwhite quail, in large expanses of light cover. But if you're hunting runners, such as ringnecks, in thick, continuous cover, you'll probably have better success with a flushing dog. A pointer won't penetrate the cover as well and will often "false point" on old scent while the bird is running ahead. Most flushers are excellent retrievers, so they're the best choice for finding downed birds in superheavy cover, such as a cattail slough.

Hunters who pursue a wide variety of upland birds, as well as waterfowl, often try to buy the perfect

"all-purpose" dog. Unfortunately, no such dog exists. You'll do better by selecting a dog well suited to your primary type of hunting, rather than one that will do a fair to poor job on several types.

Most any mutt will hunt for you. But your odds of winding up with a good bird dog increase greatly when you deal with a well-established breeder who has carefully selected the dam and sire based on their lineage and hunting skills.

Before you buy a dog, make sure you know how to care for it, both at home and in the field. If you leave a puppy unconfined in your house, plan on replacing lots of furniture, shoes and anything else it can find to chew on. Ask other hunters to recommend a good veterinarian; then take the dog in to be sure it gets all necessary treatments and vaccinations, including a shot for Lyme disease, if it's a problem in your area.

If you plan to train your own dog, get a book with specifics on your breed. Should you run into problems, seek advice from a professional trainer. Many hunters prefer to train their own dog in the basic commands – come, stay, sit, heel and kennel – and send it to a professional for advanced training, such as hand signals and holding a point. Most dogs are capable of hunting at six months of age, assuming they know the basic commands.

On the pages that follow, we'll show you the main equipment needed for care, training and handling of a hunting dog, and discuss attributes of the most popular upland bird hunting breeds.

PERMANENT KENNEL. If you plan to keep your dog outside, you'll need a kennel large enough to allow it to exercise. A 4-foot x 24-foot concrete slab makes an excellent runway. Place an insulated doghouse with a weatherproof entrance at one end of the slab, and set a 6-foot-tall wire fence on the perimeter of the slab so the dog can't dig under it. The runway is easy to hose off, and the concrete provides enough abrasion to wear down your dog's toenails.

TRAINING DEVICES. If you plan on training your own dog, consider buying (1) canvas training dummy, for teaching retrieving skills; (2) electronic shock collar, with remote control, for enforcing commands at long distance; (3) pinch collar, for teaching the "whoa" command; (4) bird scents; (5) whistle; (6) 50-foot check cord, for training a dog to stay close; (7) 5-foot leash, for teaching the "heel" command.

PORTABLE KENNEL. Used for transporting a dog in a hunting vehicle or airplane, portable kennels are available in a variety of sizes. The tendency is to choose one too large; a dog can comfortably curl up in a small space. It learns to recognize the kennel as home, so it stays more docile than a dog that is unconfined. Without a portable kennel, a muddy dog quickly makes a mess of your vehicle.

SIGNALING DEVICES. A bell (left) attached to the collar or a beeper collar (right) helps you keep track of your dog in heavy cover. If you're hunting with a pointer, a bell or beeper will tell you when the dog is on point, making it easier for you to find it. The bell will suddenly stop ringing, or the pattern or tone of beeps emitted by the collar will change.

Popular Pointing Breeds

Most pointing breeds cover more ground than the flushing/retrieving breeds (pp. 26-27), relying mainly on airborne scent to zero in on the birds. Once they detect strong-enough scent, they *point* (freeze in position), pinning down the birds and allowing the hunter time to get into position for an easy shot.

As a rule, pointers have more speed and endurance than flushers, making them a better choice for work-

ENGLISH POINTER. This breed, whose official name is simply "pointer," averages about 50 pounds. Its speedy, wide-ranging style enables it to cover ground quickly. Used extensively for southern bobwhites, it has a short coat best suited to warm climates. It is not a natural retriever, and usually must be force-trained to retrieve.

ENGLISH SETTER. A favorite among northern hunters, this breed averages 45 pounds. Most are medium-range workers, but southern-bred setters may be big runners. Its long coat is adequate for moderately cold weather, and its white color shows up well in a grouse or woodcock covert. Some retrieve naturally; others must be force-trained.

BRITTANY. Commonly called the "Brit," this short-tailed, long-haired breed is the only spaniel that points. Averaging about 35 pounds, it is the smallest pointer. The Brit's close-working habits make it suitable for most any kind of upland bird. It has a stronger retrieving instinct than an English pointer or setter.

GORDON SETTER. This long-haired Scottish import averages 50 pounds. The color of its coat explains why it was once nicknamed the black-and-tan setter. Its skills as a close-working pointer and good retriever, combined with its excellent stamina and willingness to work heavy cover, explain its recent increase in popularity.

ing very large cover parcels. They do not inspect the cover as thoroughly as flushers, but the quantity of ground they work makes up for any birds they miss.

Most pointing dogs do not have the retrieving skills of the flushing/retrieving breeds. Some hunters use a pair of dogs, backing up their pointer with a retriever to avoid losing birds, especially when hunting in heavy cover.

GERMAN WIRE-HAIRED POINTER. Also known as the Drahthaar, this bewhiskered breed makes an excellent combination upland/waterfowl dog. A close to medium worker willing to penetrate thick cover, it averages 60 pounds. The thick, wiry, water-repellent coat is bluish gray with patches of liver and brown. The tail is docked.

WIRE-HAIRED POINTING GRIFFON. Originally bred in Holland, the griffon is a slow-paced, close worker, capable of pointing upland birds and retrieving waterfowl. The stiff, protective coat is usually steel-gray or whitish gray, with chestnut splotches. Griffons average about 60 pounds and have a docked tail.

WEIMARANER. Once touted as the best all-purpose pointing breed, this German import is a close- to medium-range, moderate-paced worker with great stamina and good retrieving skills. Averaging 60 pounds, weimaraners have a short, silver-gray coat, amber- to bluish-colored eyes and a docked tail.

VIZSLA. A native of Hungary, the vizsla is relatively new to the American hunting scene. This brownish gold or rust-colored, short-haired breed has a docked tail and averages 50 pounds. A slow, close, thorough worker, the vizsla is a natural retriever and does not hesitate to go into the water.

GERMAN SHORT-HAIRED POINTER. This solid-bodied, liver-and-white or all-liver pointer averages about 55 pounds. The tail is normally docked. Most shorthairs are close, medium-paced, thorough workers, better for small fields, sloughs and woodlots than for large grass-lands. But some range as widely as an English setter. Shorthairs are good retrievers.

Popular Flushing/Retrieving Breeds

A flusher works a small parcel of cover more thoroughly than a pointer and is more likely to find and retrieve downed birds. Unlike pointers, which rely mainly on air scent, flushers follow ground scent, bulling through even the thickest tangle. In large expanses of heavy cover, where pointers have trouble pinning down birds, flushers eventually catch up with them and put them in the air. But if you don't keep up with the dog, it may flush the birds out of range.

SPRINGER SPANIEL. Often billed as the number-one pheasant breed, the springer has the ability to quickly put a bird into the air, a real asset when the birds are running. Weighing about 40 pounds, with a long, black-and-white or liver-and-white coat and a docked tail, the springer is a good retriever on land or in the water.

COCKER SPANIEL. Cockers from English lines make the best hunters. They have a long coat, usually white with black or reddish markings, and a docked tail. Named for their woodcock-hunting skills, cockers also excel for grouse and pheasant. They weigh only about 25 pounds, so they can scamper under brush impenetrable to big dogs.

BOYKIN SPANIEL. This small, little-known breed is a good upland bird flusher/retriever, and is equally adept at retrieving waterfowl. Averaging about 30 pounds, it has a moderately curly, liver- to dark-chocolate-colored coat, and a docked tail. Boykins have a mild disposition and make a good house dog.

AMERICAN WATER SPANIEL. Once a favorite waterfowling breed, the American water spaniel has slipped in popularity in recent years, probably due to declining waterfowl populations. But it remains one of the best combination waterfowl/upland dogs. Averaging 60 pounds, it has a dense, curly, liver or chocolate-brown coat.

Chocolate

Yellow

LABRADOR RETRIEVER. Most popular of all retrievers, the rugged, easy-to-train "lab" is nearly as adept at flushing, marking and fetching upland birds in heavy cover as at retrieving waterfowl. Labs have a smooth, short, burr-resistant coat that can be black, chocolate or yellow. They average 65 pounds.

CHESAPEAKE BAY RETRIEVER. Renowned for its ability to retrieve waterfowl, even in the roughest, iciest water, the burly Chesapeake is an adequate upland bird flusher and retriever. "Chessies" tend to be independent, one-man dogs. They have a coarse, oily, chocolate- to dead-grass-colored coat, and average 70 pounds.

GOLDEN RETRIEVER. The affectionate, easily trained golden retriever is just as proficient at retrieving waterfowl as at flushing and fetching upland birds, particularly pheasant, grouse and woodcock. Its wavy, long, golden outer hair has a thick undercoat, providing excellent insulation. Goldens average 65 pounds.

Hunting Techniques

Upland Bird Hunting Basics

This book provides the information you need to locate and successfully hunt every important species of upland game bird in the United States and Canada. Although the hunting techniques vary greatly depending on habits of the bird and type of terrain, a few basic principles apply to all upland bird hunting.

Before beginning your hunt, make sure your shotgun fits properly (p. 11) and practice shooting some clay targets. Study the regulations for the area where you'll be hunting to see if there are any ammunition restrictions. In some areas managed for waterfowl, for instance, steel shot is required for all upland bird hunting.

Most upland game bird hunting requires lots of walking, so if you're not in shape, get some exercise before the season opens. Take your dog afield for some long walks two or three times a week; this way, you'll both be more likely to last through opening day.

Contact state or provincial conservation agencies shortly before the hunting season opens to get current game bird counts. Most agencies conduct preseason bird censuses, and some even publish maps and detailed reports pinpointing areas of high bird density. Most upland game birds have an average life span of less than one year, so if you plan your trip based on last year's information, you could be in for a big disappointment.

Upland game birds have excellent eyesight and hearing, which are their primary means of detecting danger. They have a poorly developed sense of smell. These facts are important in planning your hunting strategy.

For instance, it pays to keep the sun at your back whenever possible. This makes it easier to see and shoot at the birds, and could make it harder for them to see you. It also helps you distinguish color, an important consideration in pheasant hunting, where only roosters can be legally taken.

A cool, humid day with light wind is ideal for upland bird hunting. The wind moves bird scent to the dog, and the moisture helps hold the scent on the vegetation. Hot, dry weather is tough on hunters and dogs. Not only does the vegetation hold little scent, dust gets in the dog's nose, affecting its ability to smell. High winds make the birds skittish. You may not hear them flush, and even if you do, they're hard to hit with the wind at their back.

Try to plan your hunt so you walk into the wind, either directly or at an angle. This way, the birds are less likely to hear or smell you, and a dog can pick up scent more easily. Because you're pushing the birds into the wind, they're likely to flush in that direction, offering you an easier shot. Be sure to keep your dog downwind of any cover where you expect to find birds.

Once you bag a bird, check its crop to see what it has been eating. This will help you determine where you should be hunting. In hot weather, gut the bird out immediately and keep it in a cooler.

Always carry a change of clothing and boots in your vehicle. This way, should you get soaked when hunting in wet grass or step into deep water at the edge of a slough, you won't have to suffer the rest of the day. It also pays to dress in layers so you can shed or add clothing as the temperature changes.

Pheasants

Upland-bird taxonomists have yet to determine with certainty what makes a pheasant a pheasant. Of the 49 pheasant species that have been identified, a few have qualities very similar to partridge or quail, but most have the following traits:

•A conspicuous difference in coloration between the cock and the hen

•Facial combs or wattles in adult cocks

•Some iridescent plumage in adult cocks

•Well-developed spurs in adult cocks

•Very long tails, especially in adult cocks

All of these differences relate to the fact that pheasants are polygamous. The gaudy coloration and showy tail help the cocks attract mates, and the spurs help them establish and defend breeding territories.

The ease in distinguishing the cock, or rooster, from the drably colored hen, even on the wing, has major game-management implications. Regulations can be set to allow harvest of only the cocks, maximizing the number of hens available to breed the following year.

Even if very few cocks remain at season's end, the birds' polygamous habits ensure that most of the hens will be bred. Fewer roosters to compete with hens for limited winter food and cover also improves the odds that hens will survive the winter.

Pheasants do not form coveys and, once they reach adulthood, are seldom found in family groups. However, large numbers of pheasants may gather in a prime feeding field or wintering area.

Most pheasant species originated in China, Japan or Mongolia. None are native to North America. Only ring-necked pheasants have been successfully established in North America, and several other species, including golden and Sichuan pheasants (below), are raised for use on private shooting preserves or for display purposes.

Golden pheasant

Sichuan pheasant

Ring-Necked Pheasant

After numerous unsuccessful stocking attempts, no one imagined that the 26 ring-necked pheasants stocked in Oregon in 1882 would result in a harvest of nearly 50,000 of the magnificent birds only a decade later.

The remarkable adaptability of this Chinese import was demonstrated time after time as the birds were introduced across the country. They're now found in 39 states and 7 Canadian provinces.

Ringneck populations in most parts of the country peaked in the 1940s, and the high levels continued into the 50s and 60s. But from the 1970s to the mid-80s, intensive farming practices took a very heavy toll, eliminating as much as 90 percent of the pheasant cover in some areas and shrinking pheasant populations accordingly. Luckily for hunters, the Conservation Reserve Program (CRP), which was initiated in 1985, has helped reverse the downward spiral (p. 46).

Ringnecks depend mainly on their eyesight and hearing to outwit hunters and predators. In tall vegetation, the birds listen for any unusual sounds and then take evasive action. Like many other game birds, they also detect approaching predators by sensing ground vibrations through pressure-sensitive pads, called *Herbst's corpuscles*, on their feet.

Known for their elusive tactics, ringnecks escape hunters by holding tight, flushing far out of gun range, or running. This explains why most accomplished pheasant hunters wouldn't think of going afield without a good bird dog. Not only will a dog point or flush the birds, it will boost your odds of retrieving downed birds in the heavy cover where pheasants are typically found.

The ringneck's diet consists mostly of small grains, supplemented by weed seeds and insects. The birds prefer corn, where it is available, but will also eat wheat, oats, soybeans, sorghum and milo. Insects, particularly grasshoppers, are commonly eaten by adults and chicks; the high protein content is needed for rapid growth.

Like most upland game birds, ringnecks are short lived. On the average, 80 percent of the birds taken by hunters were hatched the previous spring. Rarely does a pheasant live more than 2 years.

BIOLOGY AND RANGE

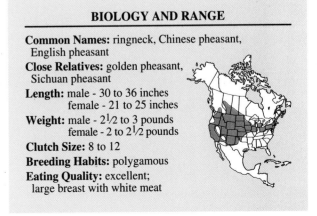

Common Names: ringneck, Chinese pheasant, English pheasant

Close Relatives: golden pheasant, Sichuan pheasant

Length: male - 30 to 36 inches
female - 21 to 25 inches

Weight: male - 2$\frac{1}{2}$ to 3 pounds
female - 2 to 2$\frac{1}{2}$ pounds

Clutch Size: 8 to 12

Breeding Habits: polygamous

Eating Quality: excellent; large breast with white meat

PHEASANT

ROOSTERS have a dark reddish copper breast with lighter copper-colored sides and back, a powder blue rump patch and a vivid white ring around the neck. The head is iridescent greenish black, with a red wattle around the eye. The brownish tail measures 18 to 26 inches in length and has numerous black bars. The bright colors make roosters attractive to hens and visible to other roosters.

HENS (inset) are dull beige, with brown and cream-colored mottling from head to tail. The mottling fades to a uniform beige toward the underside of the body. The dull colors help to camouflage hens from nest and brood predators. A hen's tail is considerably shorter than that of a rooster, ranging from 8 to 12 inches in length, but it has a similar barring pattern.

How to Determine Sex in Poor Light

CHECK the tail length on a gray day or when looking into the sun. In profile, a rooster (left) has a tail that is noticeably longer than that of a hen (right), and you may be able to see the white ring around its neck.

PHEASANT

Breeding Habits

You've probably heard the raspy "kaw kawk" call of a rooster pheasant on a spring morning or evening. The call, given at about three-minute intervals, serves to claim a territory and attract hens. Ringnecks are polygamous, so one rooster may draw a harem of a dozen or more hens. This numerical imbalance explains why roosters-only hunting regulations are effective. Even if 90 percent of all the roosters are harvested, there are enough left to breed with the remaining hens.

Roosters entice hens to breed by strutting with feathers ruffled, ear tufts erect and wattles swollen and bright red. The eggs are laid in a small, oval-shaped depression scratched into the ground by the hen and lined with grasses and possibly some feathers.

Typical pheasant nest

Hay mowers destroy many pheasant nests, and predators, particularly skunks, raccoons and snakes, eat a large number of the eggs. House cats, foxes and hawks take many of the chicks. If the nest is destroyed or raided and the hen is not killed, she will usually nest again. If the second nest fails, she may try a third. But the number of eggs decreases each time.

The eggs hatch in early summer, and the hen stays with her brood for 2 to 3 months, until the birds approach full size. By the time hunting season starts, most roosters have fully colored plumage, unless they were hatched very late in the season.

Daily Movements

Hunters can greatly improve their success by understanding the ringneck's daily movement pattern. Cover that typically holds lots of pheasants in morning and evening, for instance, may hold only a straggler or two in midday. Although movement patterns vary in different habitat types, they're fairly consistent in a given area, barring bad weather or exceptionally heavy hunting pressure. The most common scenario is as follows:

Just after sunrise, pheasants fly or walk out of their roosting cover, stopping to pick up gravel on the way to their morning feeding area, which is usually some type of crop field. After feeding for an hour or two, they move to loafing cover, such as the grassy fringe of a crop field, or they return to their roosting cover. They go out to feed again about an hour before sunset, then settle back into roosting cover for the night.

In most cases, daily movements take place within a surprisingly small area, usually no more than one-half mile in diameter. In some habitats, however, ringnecks move even less than that. For instance, they may stay in a "dirty" (weedy) cornfield all day, because there's plenty of food and ground cover. Similarly, they may stay in their roosting area all day, if there are enough weed seeds to provide adequate food.

A period of extreme cold or a heavy snow may keep the birds holding tight in dense cover for several days. Heavy dew, however, will keep birds out of the grass. On a warm winter day, they often stay out all day long, scratching for food. When hunting pressure is very heavy, they spend more time in thick cover than they otherwise would.

How to Determine Age from Spur Length

SPURS determine a rooster's approximate age. Birds less than a year old (left) have short, rounded spurs (arrow).

Those more than a year old (middle), have long, pointed spurs. Hens (right) do not have spurs.

PHEASANT

Ringneck Habitat

Ringneck pheasants are birds of the farm country. Ideal habitat consists of 55 to 70 percent crop fields, preferably corn, soybeans or small grains, with the remainder wetlands, undisturbed grasslands, small woodlots, thickets and brushy or grassy fencelines or ditches. Any of the following habitat types are likely to hold ringnecks.

STREAM CORRIDORS furnish permanent pheasant cover. Because the low-lying ground adjacent to the stream does not make good cropland, it is rarely plowed.

CATTAIL MARSHES provide excellent escape cover and winter cover. Pheasants can easily hear predators moving through the dense cover, and they can burrow under it during a severe blizzard.

DRAINAGE DITCHES may offer the only grassy cover in intensively farmed areas. Pheasants find loafing or roosting spots that are out of the wind along the slopes of the ditches.

WETLAND FRINGES make good nesting and roosting areas. Tall grasses grow there, because the ground is generally too wet to plow.

ROADSIDE DITCHES that are not routinely mowed or burned provide loafing and roosting cover. Ditches with standing water often have a growth of cattails that make good winter cover.

PHEASANT

RAILROAD RIGHTS-OF-WAY are usually allowed to grow into brushy cover that makes excellent pheasant habitat. Abandoned rights-of-way are best of all.

BRUSHY FENCELINES, especially wide strips with plenty of tall bushes or trees, make prime year-round pheasant cover.

ABANDONED FARMSTEADS offer good escape cover and winter cover. Groves and buildings break the wind, and grasses and brush that develop in open areas furnish ground cover to protect the birds from predators.

GRASSY TERRACES, intended to reduce erosion of cropland, make good loafing and roosting sites close to feeding areas.

SHELTERBELTS provide tall, dense escape cover and prevent windblown snow from clogging the birds' nostrils and suffocating them.

RETIRED CROP FIELDS that grow up to grassy cover are prime nesting areas. Unlike hay fields, they will not be mown during the nesting season.

GRASSY FRINGES of crop fields make good midday loafing sites and, if the grass is tall enough, the birds may roost there as well.

Pheasant Hunting Basics

Pheasant hunting requires some advance preparation. First, you'll need to do a little preseason scouting; it will pay big dividends later. Most fish and game departments make annual pheasant counts in late summer and publicize the results before the season opens. Study this information; then do a little research of your own. Drive around in early morning or late afternoon, watching for birds on the roadsides. When you find a promising area, talk to the landowners and ask for permission to hunt once the season begins.

Make sure you are properly outfitted (pp. 18-21). General-purpose pheasant-hunting garb consists of a hunting jacket with a good-sized game pouch, brush pants and a blaze-orange cap that makes it

easy for your companions to see you in tall cover. Comfortable boots that provide good ankle support are a must for long-distance walking.

Learn to take your time on the shot. When a gaudy rooster bursts from cover with a boisterous cackle, even veteran hunters lose their composure. If you make the mistake of rushing your shot, the bird will fly away unscathed. If you do manage to hit the bird at close range, there won't be much left of it.

Statistics show that more than 3 times as many pheasants are taken in the first half of the season as in the last. That's because most hunters want to get the "dumb" young birds. Hunting pressure is normally heaviest on opening weekend and tapers off steadily through the season.

Once the young birds are "educated," hunting becomes much tougher, but the competition for hunting spots decreases greatly. For this reason, many experienced hunters prefer the late season.

Because the birds' behavior changes so much over the season, your success will improve greatly if you learn to tailor your hunting tactics accordingly.

PHEASANT

Tips for Early-Season Pheasant Hunting

Early in the season you can find pheasants most anywhere, including grass fields, cattail sloughs, cornfields, roadside ditches and brushy draws. They may be in light or heavy cover. Public hunting areas, though crowded, produce a lot of birds. Here are some early-season hunting tips:

•Wait until the initial opening-day barrage is over, and then go back through areas that have already been hunted. Birds flushed by hunters move between different fields throughout the day.

•Look for dense or hard-to-reach cover that would discourage all but die-hard hunters.

•Work short-grass loafing areas adjacent to cropfields. These spots "burn out" early, however, and then hold only hens.

•For the close-range shooting likely in early season, most hunters prefer improved-cylinder- or modified-choke shotguns with size 6 or 7½ shot.

Tips for Late-Season Pheasant Hunting

Many veteran pheasant hunters would rather hunt in late season than fight the early-season crowds. Although the birds "wise up" in a hurry, you can still have good success in late season if you proceed as follows:

•Look for wetlands and other very dense cover areas. As the season progresses, birds seek heavier and heavier cover.

•Try to find offbeat spots, such as a small clump of trees and brush in the middle of a section. Most hunters are not willing to walk this far to work a small piece of cover, so these spots sometimes load up with birds.

•Check any road ditches with dense cover, such as cattails or horsetail. Ditches give the birds easy access to the gravel needed to grind food in their gizzard.

•Work grassy ditches, sloughs or other brushy cover adjacent to newly harvested crop fields. If you watch as a cornfield is being picked, for instance, you'll often see birds flying into these areas.

•Keep noise to a minimum. Pheasants rely heavily on their hearing to detect danger and will often flush hundreds of yards ahead if you slam your car door or yell at your hunting partner or dog. The birds get jumpier as the season progresses. Noise is not as big a problem on windy days.

•For long-range shots often required in late season, use a modified- or full-choke shotgun with size 4 or 5 shot.

Try short-grass loafing areas near crop fields in early season

Hunt out-of-the-way cover in late season

PHEASANT

Hunting Pheasants in Rowcrop Fields

Today's clean, well-manicured rowcrop fields are less than ideal for pheasant hunting. The birds often begin running out one end of the field soon after hunters walk into the other.

In years past, hunting a rowcrop field was much like hunting a block of grassy cover. The crops were much shorter and there was considerably more weedy ground cover than is the case today. Pheasants held much longer, so one or two hunters could work the field and have a good chance of flushing birds at close range.

If you're lucky, you may still find an occasional dirty field; if you do, it will probably hold more birds than other nearby fields.

The open rows in today's clean fields make perfect running lanes for pheasants. The only practical way to hunt such a field is by driving it with a group of hunters and placing posters at the end.

Some hunters who own good bird dogs refuse to hunt clean fields because they're not conducive to good dog work. Even a well-trained dog finds it hard to resist chasing a rooster down an open corn row. But in early season, when a high percentage of the crops are still standing, there may be no other choice, because that's where the birds are.

Don't ignore crop stubble, especially if it has scattered weed patches. The stubble makes a prime feeding area and is usually high enough to conceal a sneaking rooster.

Hunting rowcrop fields is most productive the first and last two hours of the day, although they may hold pheasants anytime. Avoid hunting these fields in windy weather. The rustling leaves are so noisy that you may not hear the birds flush. And you probably won't be able to hear the footsteps of your hunting partners or your dog.

PHEASANT

Tips for Hunting Pheasants in Rowcrop Fields

PINPOINT midday cover by watching where the birds fly when they leave the rowcrop field after their morning feeding period.

SEND the outside driver ahead of the drivers in the row-crop field. This helps prevent birds from flying out ahead, and, if they do, the outside driver may have a shot.

WALK crosswise through the rows when hunting alone in tall rowcrops. This way, you can peer down one row at a time to surprise the birds.

POSITION posters along the sides of the field, as well as the ends, to block as many escape routes as possible.

When hunting rowcrop fields, follow these simple guidelines:

•Try to drive manageable strips, no more than two hundred yards wide. It's very difficult to pin birds down in a huge field, no matter how many hunters in your party.

•Small parties can work big crop fields by concentrating on edge rows, always pushing them toward the corners.

•Don't attempt to hunt a rowcrop or stubble field unless you have posters at the end, preferably at intervals of no more than 60 yards. Posters must remain silent and as inconspicuous as possible, so as not to alert the birds. Otherwise, they may flush prematurely.

•Posters and drivers should wear a blaze-orange cap when hunting crop fields; this way, they can see one another more easily in the tall cover.

•Drivers should walk into the wind; this way, the birds are less likely to hear them coming, and dogs can pick

up scent more easily. A favorable wind also helps the dogs hear running pheasants.

•Position drivers at 15- to 20-yard intervals, and make sure the middle drivers stay a little behind the outer drivers; this way, the birds usually funnel toward the middle. Drivers should zigzag a little to keep the birds from stopping or doubling back.

•If there is thick cover adjacent to the field, include it in your drive.

•Be alert when drivers approach posters; birds running down the rows will be trapped near the end and many may flush at once. Never shoot at birds flying low over the field; there could be another hunter in the line of fire.

•Flushers generally work best in open crop fields; pointers may have difficulty pinning the birds down. In cut fields, however, birds often hold under fallen leaves and stalks, where pointers can pin them down more easily.

PHEASANT

Hunting Pheasants in Wetlands

Wetlands often provide the heaviest, most secure cover available to pheasants. The twisted cattails, brush clumps and marsh grasses make it almost impossible for a predator to approach unnoticed and offer excellent protection from severe winter storms.

Pheasants also congregate in wetlands to escape hunting pressure. The impenetrable cover can be a nightmare for hunters and dogs, so these areas are often passed over by all but the most avid hunters.

The most productive wetland areas are adjacent to crop fields. The combination of an easy food source and good cover makes for ideal pheasant habitat.

The usual technique for hunting a wetland is to work the high spots, such as outside edges where water meets land, and any islands in the middle. If you can find a well-worn deer trail, walking will be much easier.

Don't hesitate to hunt in a few inches of water; deeper areas seldom hold pheasants. If possible, have a partner approach from the opposite side so you flush birds toward each other.

A tough, close-working flusher, such as a Labrador or Chesapeake, is a must for hunting wetlands. It will root out birds that decide to hunker down in the dense cover. And when you drop a bird, the dog won't hesitate to crawl into the thickest tangle to retrieve it.

Lightweight hip boots or waders are recommended for most types of wetland hunting. Even if you're hunting high ground around the edges, you may want to reach lightly hunted islands or retrieve birds that fall into deep water.

You're most likely to find pheasants in wetlands in midday, in stormy weather and when hunting pressure in the surrounding area is heavy. But wetlands hold a few birds most anytime. More and more pheasants gather in wetland areas as the hunting season progresses. When crops are harvested and grassy cover gets matted down by snow, wetlands may be the only cover remaining.

Tips for Hunting Pheasants in Wetlands

LOOK for wetlands within crop fields. They hold loafing pheasants in midday and, if they have a heavy growth of cattails, make good spots in late season.

WAIT until wetlands freeze over so you can walk around more easily. Make sure there are at least 4 inches of ice, and avoid walking near weed clumps, where the ice is weaker.

HUNT Waterfowl Production Areas (WPAs), federally-owned wetlands with plenty of grassy cover that is ideal for nesting waterfowl, and for pheasants.

WORK both sides of ditches and other waterways by crossing at beaver dams. After hunting an area a few times, you'll know exactly where the dams are located.

Hunting Pheasants in Tall Grass

Most tall grass fields in pheasant country are a result of federal land-retirement programs intended to reduce crop production and combat soil erosion. Farmers receive government payments for keeping their land idle. After the land is taken out of production, it is planted with a variety of grasses to stabilize the soil while providing cover for wildlife.

The "Soil Bank" program, in effect from 1957 to 1963, is credited for greatly improving pheasant populations throughout the plains states. In west-central Minnesota, for instance, pheasant counts doubled within two years of the program's inception. Six years after the program ended, the pheasant population had plummeted to one-fifteenth the level in peak program years. The Conservation Reserve Program (CRP), which began in 1985, has also been very successful in bolstering pheasant populations. In Iowa, for example, the pheasant harvest increased about 50 percent during the program's first six years.

CRP fields make better pheasant habitat than hay fields. They provide ideal nesting and roosting cover and, unlike hay fields, are not mowed around nesting time. Mowing destroys the nests or kills the chicks. The government may grant permission to mow CRP fields, however, in cases of severe drought that results in a food shortage for cattle.

Most grass fields contain little pheasant food, so the ones near crop fields are likely to hold the most birds. Height and density of cover are also important. Tall, dense fields are much better than short, sparse ones.

You can find birds in grass fields throughout the hunting season, as long as a heavy snowfall doesn't flatten the cover too much and force pheasants into brushy cover, woodlots or wetlands.

Tips for Hunting Pheasants in Tall Grass

SELECT large, dense CRP fields (left), preferably those with crop fields on at least two sides. Fields with sparse or short grasses (right) hold fewer birds.

HUNT the edges of any small creeks or drainage ditches flowing through a grass field. The varied cover holds more birds than grass alone.

Pheasants usually fly out of grass fields within two hours after sunrise, then return in mid- to late morning, after they finish feeding. They normally fly out to feed again in late afternoon. Spend some time watching them with binoculars to get a better idea of their daily movement schedule.

Dog work in grassy cover is best on humid days, because moist grass holds scent better than dry grass. But if the grass is too wet, pheasants won't stay in it.

A good flusher is especially important in hunting tall grass cover, where there is nothing to stop the birds from running and downed birds are notoriously hard to find. Some pointers can learn to follow and relocate running birds, but others find it hard to pin them down; when they're pointing, the bird is running ahead.

With a big group of hunters, you can drive a large grass field much as you would a crop field. Start at one edge of the field, spread out at about 15-yard intervals and start walking. When you reach the end of the field, move over and take another swath in the opposite direction. Continue until the entire field has been covered. Posters can be used, but are not as essential as in hunting crop fields; in the heavier cover, the birds are not as likely to run to the end of the field. As in crop field hunting, all hunters should wear blaze-orange caps.

Another effective way to hunt tall grass, especially for one or two hunters, is to start on the downwind side and follow your dog. Don't try to tell the dog where to go; allow it to work out every scent trail. Make sure, however, to work the edges, especially those adjacent to cropfields.

If you don't have a dog, the only option is to hunt very slowly, stopping periodically to make the birds nervous. On a quiet day, you may be able to hear birds moving through the grass.

LOOK for brush, trees or any high or dense spots within large expanses of grass. Birds flying into a grass field will seek out these heavy-cover areas.

WORK the edges of tall grass fields when hunting alone or in a small party. Edge cover holds the most birds, and the edge helps confine them on one side.

Hunting Pheasants in the Snow

A heavy snow immediately changes the way pheasants behave, forcing you to modify your hunting tactics. You'll no longer find birds in light cover, such as grass fields, because snow mats down the vegetation. Instead, look for them in spots that offer secure overhead cover and protection from the wind, such as dense cattail marshes, brushy draws and woodlots.

The first snowfall of the year makes birds nervous. Most of them have never seen snow and it seems to confuse them. You'll often see them standing out in the open or scurrying across roads when the snow starts to fall.

The birds frequently allow themselves to become snowed in beneath the cover. Sometimes they will stay in their hiding spots for a day or two after a snowstorm has subsided. But, in most cases, they come out to feed on the first calm, sunny day following a snowstorm.

Although pheasants tend to be spookier when snow covers the ground, they're more concentrated and easier to find than they were in early season, because there is much less usable feeding area and hiding cover. Birds congregate in areas where they can find food most easily. Sometimes a prime feeding area will attract birds from several sections of land.

Watch for groups of feeding birds as you drive around, and look for feeding sign, such as ground scratchings, as you hunt. Be sure to work any brushy cover, such as willow clumps, plum thickets and shelterbelts, near feeding areas.

Always look for fresh pheasant tracks to determine if birds are using an area. With a little practice, you'll be able to distinguish the tracks of a rooster from those of a hen; a rooster's tail usually leaves a drag mark in the snow.

Following rooster tracks can be a productive hunting method, but only right after a snowfall. Otherwise, you won't be able to determine if the tracks are fresh.

Most hunters prefer to use flushing dogs in heavy snow. Birds hunkered down in a snow clump emit very little scent. A pointer, which relies mainly on air scent, may run right past the clump; a flusher, which trails ground scent, will stick his nose into it.

Many hunters make the mistake of dressing too warmly when hunting in snow. A heavy parka will cause you to sweat when you walk, and you'll get colder than if you wore a lighter coat. Heavy felt pack boots also make your feet sweat; lightweight, insulated Gore-Tex® boots keep them warm and dry.

When hunting in snow in late season, use a full- or modified-choke shotgun and size 4 or 5 shot, because the birds tend to flush wild. Some hunters even use 2 shot for extra distance. When birds get this spooky, it's difficult to hunt alone successfully. If a partner approaches from the opposite direction, however, one of you will probably get some shooting.

Tips for Hunting Pheasants in the Snow

WORK tall clumps of brush, such as red osier dogwood, when hunting in the snow. Large groups of pheasants often congregate in such spots.

PINPOINT pheasant concentrations by looking for them after a snowfall. Clear weather brings the birds out, and they're easy to see against the white backdrop.

WEAR waxed pants when hunting in deep snow. The wax finish repels snow, and, even if the snow sticks and melts, it won't soak into the fabric.

CHECK for fresh footprints (human and dog) in the snow to determine if the spot you wish to hunt has been recently hunted. Without snow, you would not be able to tell.

DOWN AND BACK. This method is effective in strip cover that is too wide to cover in one swath. The technique's name is self-explanatory. In the case of a railroad track, for instance, a hunter simply walks down one side and back on the opposite side. The same technique could be used to hunt road ditches, drainage ditches or parallel windbreaks.

Hunting Pheasants in Strip Cover

Strip cover includes any linear cover, such as road ditches, drainage ditches, stream corridors, fencerows, windbreaks and railroad tracks. In many prime agricultural areas, strip cover is practically the only pheasant cover that remains. Strip cover bordering crop fields is generally more productive than that which is isolated.

This type of cover is ideal for a lone hunter and is probably the best choice for the hunter who does not have a dog. The narrow width improves your odds of flushing any birds that are present.

Close-working dogs are the best choice in strip cover. The birds are not likely to evade a good dog in a narrow cover strip, so their only escape tactic is to run ahead. If the dog pushes them too hard, they'll flush wild.

When using a dog, be sure to walk along the downwind edge of strip cover. This gives the dog the best chance to scent birds.

Hunting strip cover requires some planning; otherwise, you'll wind up backtracking through cover you've already hunted to get back to your vehicle. The idea is to plan your hunt so you're always working fresh cover.

Tips for Hunting Pheasants in Strip Cover

DROP OFF a bicycle or motorbike a mile or two upwind of your starting point; drive your hunting vehicle to the starting point, hunt back to the bike, and then ride the bike back to the vehicle.

PHEASANT

OPPOSITE ENDS. This method enables hunters to approach from opposite directions without having to backtrack. In this situation, two hunters walk toward each other from opposite sides of a section. After they meet, they walk out along the strip in the foreground (arrows), and then hunt road ditches back to their vehicle.

LEAPFROGGING. This technique, which requires at least two hunters, is ideal for hunting railroad tracks or other long stretches of strip cover. The usual strategy is for the first hunter to start at the downwind point of the stretch, while the second drives upwind to the next road, parks the vehicle, and works the next section. When the first hunter reaches the vehicle, he drives around to leapfrog the second, and so on.

SEND one hunter ahead to block if you suspect a bird is running ahead of you in strip cover. When the bird realizes it's trapped between two hunters, it has no choice but to flush.

WORK a creek bottom or other wide strip cover with one hunter and a dog in the middle, and another hunter along the *downwind* edge. The upwind edge is usually not as productive, because the birds tend to fly with the wind.

Partridge

Partridges are not native to North America, but two Eurasian imports, the gray, or Hungarian, partridge and the chukar partridge, have been widely stocked and have established healthy populations. Two other species closely related to the chukar, the Barbary partridge and the red-legged partridge, have also been introduced in some western states, but they have interbred with chukars and are no longer distinguishable as separate species in this region.

Medium-size birds ranging from 1 to 1½ pounds, the introduced partridges resemble quail in many respects. They're monogamous, form coveys, often roost in a circle, usually renest if their original brood is lost and do not perform elaborate mating rituals.

As a rule, partridges prefer lighter cover than most other kinds of upland game birds. This trait evidently allows them to spot approaching predators. Even without heavy cover, they have an uncanny ability to survive severe winters.

Partridges are most closely related to pheasants, but they're easy to distinguish because of their shorter, more rounded tail and considerably smaller size. They also lack the leg spurs. Another difference: they are much less territorial than pheasants during the breeding season.

HUNGARIAN PARTRIDGE have a cinnamon-colored mask, a light brownish back with cream-colored streaks, chestnut bars on the flanks, and a gray breast. In males, the breast often has a distinct horseshoe mark (opposite).

54

PARTRIDGE

Hungarian Partridge

Although gray partridge is the official name for this species, most hunters call it the Hungarian partridge. or simply "hun."

As the name suggests, the bird was imported from Hungary and other parts of Europe. The first successful plants were in Washington and California during the late 1800s to early 1900s. A 1908 stocking in Alberta is credited with establishing huns in the Great Plains, which is now their major stronghold.

Males make a raspy, metallic-sounding "keee-uk" (the rusty gate call) to establish their breeding territory and attract females. The male's mating ritual consists of a combination of neck stretching, strutting, circling and walking with his head low to the ground. Mating takes place in spring, from mid-April through May.

Cool, damp weather following the hatch takes a heavy toll on the young birds. On the average, 30 percent of them live to their second year. A typical fall covey consists of about 80 percent young birds and the rest adults, including the parents and possibly a few others with no broods.

Huns have the remarkable ability to survive harsh winter conditions by roosting in the snow, using its insulating properties as a substitute for heavy vegetative cover. They also form a roosting ring, much like bobwhite quail (p. 95), to preserve body heat. This behavior explains why they can thrive in intensively farmed areas where pheasant populations have declined. It also explains why they do not have to move far to find winter cover. But even huns cannot survive extremely severe winters with heavy snow cover. They cannot reach food beneath the heavy snow blanket.

On a typical day, huns will feed in a small-grain field for an hour or two in early morning, walk to a short-grass field where they will loaf during midday, then feed again in late afternoon. They fly to roosting areas just before sunset.

Even where huns are plentiful, few hunters specifically go after them. Most are taken incidentally by sharptail and pheasant hunters. Because of the hun's minimal cover needs, it's difficult to predict where they'll be at what time of day. Expect to find a covey just about anywhere – even in a plowed field.

MALE Hungarian partridge (left) have a chestnut-colored horseshoe on the breast. In females (right), the breast normally is a uniform grayish color, but it may have a less conspicuous horseshoe.

BIOLOGY AND RANGE

Common Names: hun, hunkie, Bohemian partridge
Close Relatives: chukar, red-legged and Barbary partridge
Length: 12 to 14 inches
Weight: 12 to 16 ounces
Clutch Size: 10 to 20
Breeding Habits: monogamous
Eating Quality: excellent; breast meat is moderately dark

Small-grain fields protected by windbreaks are ideal for huns

Hun Habitat

Huns prefer open farm country ranging from flat prairie to gently rolling hills. Ideally, about 65 percent of the acreage should be in small grains, such as wheat, oats and barley; the rest, in native grasslands, hay fields, and retired crop fields with grass less than 2 feet tall. The latter habitats are used not only for nesting, but also for raising the brood and roosting. Other cover used for these purposes includes roadsides and grassy fringes around woodlots and fence rows. Huns are also found in sagebrush/grassland habitat with small-grain fields nearby. Woodlands seldom hold huns.

Farmsteads make ideal hun habitat. They offer protection from wind and snow and a source of food. Trees and brushy hedges form windbreaks, and the birds can usually find grain around the farmyard and in harvested crop fields trampled down by cattle. In a North Dakota winter survey, 54 of 59 coveys spotted were near farmsteads.

Brushy farm groves draw huns

The best hun habitat receives low to moderate rainfall. The birds get enough water from their food. This explains why huns are sometimes found in the same arid habitat as chukars.

A radio-tagging study conducted in Iowa revealed that most huns are found within 50 feet of the edge of the cover they are using. By staying this close, they can fulfill all of their daily needs with a minimum of movement, reducing the chances that they'll be seen by predators or hunters. Experienced hunters know they can improve their odds by confining their efforts to field edges.

Techniques for Hunting Huns

Many an upland-game-bird hunter has watched in disbelief after emptying his gun at a flock of huns and not bringing down a feather. When the sky is full of birds, it would seem impossible to miss, so the tendency is to "flock shoot."

Exploding from cover en masse is a survival adaptation intended to confuse predators. If you are to become a successful "predator" you must resist the tendency to flock shoot and learn to pick out individual birds.

What makes hunting for huns so difficult is their ability to use such a wide variety of cover. With the coveys spread over so much area, your odds of finding one are much lower than would be the case with coveys of bobwhite quail, for instance, whose locational patterns are much more predictable. Adding to the difficulty are their habits of running to evade hunters and dogs and flushing wildly out of gun range.

Most veteran hunters have established a "milk run" of spots known to hold huns. A typical run might include an abandoned farmstead, a strip of grassy cover along a drainage ditch, a grassy railroad right-of-way, and a wheat-stubble field. The spots that hold huns one year are likely to hold them the next, assuming the habitat does not change too much. Concentrating your efforts on these prime spots will maximize your odds, especially in years when the population is low.

You'll seldom find huns in cattail marshes, dense brush, tall-grass fields, woodland edges or other heavy cover. But they're commonly found along the grassy fringes of these areas.

Close-working pointing breeds, such as Brittany spaniels, are a good all-around choice for huns. Wider-ranging breeds, such as English pointers, are better for working prairie or other open lands. They cover a lot of ground quickly and may be able to pin down a covey while the hunter approaches. But if the dog pushes the birds too hard or is not staunch on the point, the covey will flush out of range. Close-working flushers are preferred in farmsteads, strip cover, or other spots where the birds' location is more obvious.

When a covey flushes, the birds chirp excitedly. Watch closely; they normally will fly no more than 300 yards and sometimes less than 100. Keep following them; a covey usually stays together, and you can flush it two or three times. How tight the birds hold on successive flushes depends on the density of the cover. If it's very light, you probably won't get close enough for a shot; if it's heavy, you may be able to walk right up to them. If the covey breaks up, follow singles and doubles. They're more likely to hold tight than is an entire covey.

Because the chances of multiple long shots are high, a 12-gauge pump or semi-automatic shotgun with a modified choke is the best all-around choice for huns. A double-barrel with modified and improved-cylinder chokes is also a good selection. Use high-power shells with 6 or 7½ shot.

WATCH for huns along gravel roads after sunrise and before sunset. This is a quick way of determining where hun numbers are high.

Tips for Hunting Huns

HUNT dried-up wetlands for huns. The heavy vegetation that develops in the fertile basin may be the best cover available.

LOOK for open-country huns around man-made features that provide a windbreak, such as an old barn, farm machinery or an old fence.

WORK the edges of wheat-stubble fields early and late in the day. Birds that spent the day in heavier cover move into the stubble to feed, and they're more likely to feed near the edge of the field than in the middle.

CHUKAR PARTRIDGE have a distinctive black mask that passes through the eye. The mask connects to a black collar that borders the whitish face. Parallel dark bars cover the flanks. The breast and crown are gray; the back, grayish brown; the bill and legs, red. The sexes are identical in coloration, but males are slightly larger.

PARTRIDGE

Chukar Partridge

The chukar gets its name from its unique rallying call, a shrill "chuk-chuk-chuk-chukara." Males also use this call to mark their territory during the breeding season.

A native of India and the Middle East, the chukar was introduced into 42 states and 6 provinces from the late 1800s through the mid-1950s. Introductions were most successful in dry, mountainous, sparsely vegetated areas of the West and Northwest, terrain very similar to their native habitat. The first chukar hunting season was held in Nevada in 1947.

The chukar's well-known habit of running when alarmed relates to the open ground it inhabits. With very little vegetation dense enough to provide hiding cover, running is their best escape tactic. They rely heavily on their eyesight and hearing to detect danger. Often, a sentry posts itself atop a boulder or rocky outcrop where it can easily spot approaching predators or hunters and warn the covey. When the birds run, they almost always go uphill, but when they flush, they fly downhill.

A chukar eats mainly seeds and grasses, particularly cheat grass. Additional food items include grasshoppers and other insects and, when they're available, small grains, such as wheat and oats. The life span of a chukar is very short. On the average, only 10 percent of the fall population consists of adult birds.

Long-term weather patterns affect chukar population levels. Brood size is directly related to the amount of rainfall. Broods are smaller, for instance, during drought periods, when there is a shortage of grasses and other foods. Deep, crusted snow also reduces survival by preventing the birds from feeding.

Compared to most other upland game birds, chukars are highly mobile. Tagging studies have shown that they can move as far as 38 miles over the course of the year. Although they seldom travel more than a mile in any one day, the ability to move long distances allows them to seek out the best available habitat.

Chukars have an elaborate early-spring mating ritual in which the male struts and waltzes to entice the female to breed. A covey usually consists of 15 to 20 birds, but sometimes individual coveys combine to form larger ones with as many as 40 birds.

BIOLOGY AND RANGE

Common Names: red-legged partridge, redlegs, rock partridge
Close Relatives: gray partridge
Length: 12 to 15 inches
Weight: 1 to $1^1/2$ pounds
Clutch Size: 10 to 20
Breeding Habits: monogamous
Eating Quality: excellent; much like Hungarian partridge

Mountain slopes covered by cheat grass (inset) make ideal chukar habitat

Chukar Habitat

Chukars thrive in arid, mountainous country laced with brushy creekbeds. In the western United States, they're found mainly at altitudes of 4,000 to 11,000 feet in regions with an annual rainfall of less than 10 inches. South-facing slopes heated by the sun are most likely to hold chukars in the morning and on cool days. On hot days, you'll often find them near water holes or along brushy stream courses.

The birds commonly nest beneath bushes, trees or sagebrush, or in crevices between rocks. The nest is merely a small depression scratched into the ground and lined with leaves, grasses and feathers. Good nesting habitat is usually on a south-facing slope, and protects the birds from the top and from all sides but the front.

Winter habitat is much like summer habitat, but at a lower elevation (6,000 feet or less) where the snow is not as deep and there is more brushy cover. A heavy blanket of snow hampers their ability to scratch for seeds.

Techniques for Hunting Chukars

One easy way to find chukars is to locate likely habitat and spend a little time listening for their calls. You can entice the birds to "talk" with a chukar call.

Hunters who understand that chukars usually run uphill when danger threatens can use this habit to their advantage. With a pair of hunters walking a mountain slope (opposite), birds running uphill to escape the bottom hunter will usually flush when they encounter the top hunter.

Often, you'll see the birds running ahead of you. If this happens, you may be able to sneak over a crest, move ahead a few hundred yards, then work back down toward them. This tactic usually forces the birds to flush, because they will not run downhill. Another effective technique is to rush the running birds to get close enough for a shot. If a covey flushes out of range, try shooting into the air anyway. When they land, they will be more likely to hold tight so you can get close enough for a shot.

Once you find a covey, note the elevation, because other coveys will probably be at about the same elevation. As a rule, a covey will break up when it flushes, giving you an opportunity to pursue singles and doubles. The birds will generally hold tighter the second time.

Chukar hunters often debate the value of a dog. If your dog tends to run wild in open country, leave it at home. But a good pointing dog is invaluable for locating singles once a covey has broken up, finding cripples, and retrieving birds that drop into gullies or other hard-to-reach spots.

Short-haired pointers, such as German shorthairs, are popular with chukar hunters; long-haired breeds can easily become overheated in the desertlike terrain. A flushing dog is best kept at heel until you spot some birds. Then, release it to break up the covey.

Be sure to carry a first-aid kit (p. 21) for your dog when hunting chukars. Sharp rocks, thorns and cactus

PARTRIDGE

spines can inflict some bad cuts. A snakebite kit is also recommended. Some hunters outfit their dogs with leather boots to protect their feet.

The birds are not hard to bring down, but the open country often means long-distance shooting. The best all-around chukar gun is a 16- to 20-gauge pump or semi-automatic with a full or modified choke. In double barrels, however, many hunters prefer an improved-cylinder/modified combo, because there is a chance of close flushes. High-power shells with size 7½ shot are recommended. Often, hunters will back up their 7½s with one or two 6 shot. A sling on your shotgun makes it much easier to carry when you are climbing the steep slopes.

A good pair of lightweight boots with lug soles, steel toes and strong ankle support are a must for walking in this steep, rocky terrain. Lightweight, breathable clothing is recommended until the weather turns cold; otherwise, you'll work up too much of a sweat climbing the steep slopes.

Tips for Hunting Chukars

HUNT down the slope to reach known or suspected coveys. If you push the birds uphill, they're much more likely to run.

LISTEN for chukars in early morning. When you hear the call, which carries for up to a mile on a still morning, look for the birds with binoculars. Even if you don't see them, walk to the spot where the call seemed to originate.

WORK a mountain slope by spreading out vertically. The top hunter should stay well above and slightly ahead of the bottom one. The birds usually flush downhill, often giving both hunters a shot.

LOOK for chukars near river corridors, particularly in dry weather. Bird numbers tend to be higher in these areas, because of the easy access to water.

Grouse

This diverse and widely distributed family includes three broad types of game birds: prairie grouse, forest grouse and ptarmigan. All of the grouse species present in North America are native, not introduced.

Prairie grouse (sage and sharptail grouse, greater and lesser prairie chicken) inhabit sprawling plains and grasslands. Forest grouse (ruffed, spruce and blue grouse) are normally associated with northern forests, sometimes in mountainous terrain. Ptarmigan are found on the tundra or in alpine habitat.

All grouse, with the exception of the ptarmigan, are polygamous. Colorful, ritualized mating displays, which include various forms of jumping, strutting, drumming or calling by the male, combined with inflating of bright-colored air sacs on the neck in many species, are intended to defend territories and win females. Prairie grouse conduct communal displays, which include as many as 50 males, on traditional breeding areas, called dancing grounds, or *leks*.

Grouse usually produce only one brood per year and, unlike many other upland game birds, will seldom renest if the original brood is lost to predators or cold, wet weather.

In late fall and winter, prairie grouse and ptarmigan congregate in large flocks, or *packs*, that may number in the hundreds of birds. With so many eyes and ears, the pack provides an excellent means of defense on the open prairie. These packs are extremely hard to approach and usually flush well out of gun range.

Forest grouse, however, are loners. The hen stays with the young until they reach almost full size, but the birds then scatter, and young males establish their own territories.

Grouse are easy to distinguish from other kinds of upland game birds. On others, the feathering on the legs stops short of the knee, but on grouse, it extends at least to the base of the toes. The males of most grouse species have colorful combs above the eyes that become more prominent at breeding time. They do not have leg spurs. In winter, most grouse species develop tiny comblike projections, called *pectinations*, on the edges of their toes. The pectinations make it easier for them to grip icy branches and, under some conditions, may act as snowshoes, helping to support the bird's weight.

RUFFED GROUSE get their name from the conspicuous *ruff*, a patch of black feathers on the neck. The tail has a distinct dark band near the end. Two different color phases, gray and red (inset), may occur in the same family.

Ruffed Grouse

Sometimes called "drummers" because of the male's habit of beating its wings rapidly and loudly to stake out its breeding territory, ruffed grouse are one of the most studied yet least understood game birds. They're called "ruffs" or "partridge" in many areas, and "pa'tridge" in the New England states. But the latter terms are misnomers; the only true partridges in North America are the gray and chukar, both introduced species.

The drumming, which is done while the male is perched on a favorite "drumming log," is most often heard in spring. But it's also common in fall and may be heard throughout the year. The sound has been likened to an old one-cylinder tractor starting slowly, then gradually speeding up. Each drumbeat is created by rapid wing movement and is a miniature version of a sonic boom.

Drumming keeps rival males away and attracts females. Breeding takes place from March to May, depending on latitude. The hen tends the eggs for about 3 weeks and stays with the chicks through early fall, until they are almost full-grown. The brood then disperses, with some of the birds moving as far as 10 miles from their rearing areas to establish their own home range. This behavior is commonly referred to as the *fall shuffle*.

Once a male grouse locates a suitable drumming site that has not already been claimed by an older male, he will not stray far from it. He spends the rest of his life in an area no larger than 10 acres. A female's home range is larger, up to 40 acres, and often overlaps that of two or more males.

Ruffed grouse are native to almost all of Canada south of the treeline, and to 39 states, mainly in the North and mountainous regions of the East and West. They have been planted in Newfoundland, Nevada, Oklahoma and Colorado.

BIOLOGY AND RANGE

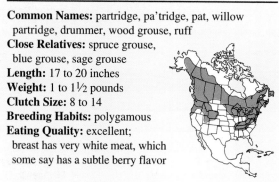

Common Names: partridge, pa'tridge, pat, willow partridge, drummer, wood grouse, ruff
Close Relatives: spruce grouse, blue grouse, sage grouse
Length: 17 to 20 inches
Weight: 1 to 1½ pounds
Clutch Size: 8 to 14
Breeding Habits: polygamous
Eating Quality: excellent; breast has very white meat, which some say has a subtle berry flavor

GROUSE

Female

Male

The species has two distinct color phases (opposite). Although both phases are found throughout the range, the gray phase is most common in the northern part of the range and at high altitudes. The red phase (also called brown phase) is more prevalent in the southern part of the range and at lower altitudes. Biologists have identified 12 separate races of ruffed grouse, all with slightly different coloration.

In most of the ruffed grouse range, with the main exception of the eastern states, populations are highly cyclical. In peak years, numbers may be 15 times as high as in lean years. These cycles, which are about 10 years in duration, have been attributed to everything from forest fires to sunspots.

Perhaps the most likely explanation is the natural predator-prey cycle. Many predators, such as hawks, owls, foxes and bobcats prey on snowshoe hares as well as grouse. Hares are prolific breeders, and when conditions are right, their population explodes. Because the predators have plenty of food, predation on grouse decreases, allowing their population to build up. Eventually, the hares become so numerous that there is not enough food to support them, so their population crashes. Then, predation switches to the grouse, causing their numbers to dwindle.

A grouse's best defense against predation is keeping its movements to a minimum, especially when it's contrasted against a backdrop of snow. The only time of year when grouse make long-distance movements is during the fall dispersal period, when the "crazy flight" phenomenon causes headaches for homeowners in wooded areas as birds sometimes fly through their windows.

Ruffs have an unusual habit that protects them from predators in winter. They fly into deep, soft snow at high speed, often penetrating several feet. Then they burrow ahead, sometimes more than 10 feet, stopping a few inches beneath the surface of the snow.

SEX can be determined by examining the tail band. Males (bottom tail), have a solid band around the entire margin. In females (top tail), the two center feathers do not have a distinct band.

They roost in these burrows and can easily burst out when threatened. The insulating blanket of snow also conserves body heat. In cold weather, grouse often stay in their burrows all day. Some grouse are injured or killed when they attempt to fly into ice-crusted snow, however.

Although ruffs are not as vocal as many other game birds, the hen often clucks to let the chicks know where she is. When she detects a predator, she emits a short, high-pitched squeal that causes the chicks to head for the nearest cover and freeze until the threat passes. If a predator approaches the chicks, the hen feigns a broken wing to lure it away. Or, she may puff up her feathers and charge an intruder.

Grouse do most of their feeding early and late in the day. In midday, they usually seek heavier cover and move very little, making hunting more difficult. Confining their activities to dim-light periods makes it more difficult for predators to spot them.

When in danger, ruffed grouse, with the exception of older males, are less likely to run than pheasants or partridge. Often, they'll simply hop up into a tree, or, in heavier cover, they'll freeze. They can reduce the amount of scent they emit by scrunching tight to the ground and compressing their feathers. Depending on how heavily they're hunted, they can be extremely wary or indifferent to danger.

Aspen buds are a major food for ruffed grouse, because of their high nutritional value. The buds are particularly important in winter, when snow covers most other foods. Aspen grow in clones, groups of trees of the same sex, and grouse prefer buds of male trees, which are larger and higher in nutrition than those of female trees. If you consistently find grouse in a certain aspen stand, it's probably a clone of male trees. Buds of trees more than 30 years old provide more nourishment than those of younger trees. Grouse also eat buds, leaves and twigs from other kinds of trees, as well as fruits, berries and clover.

Ruffed Grouse Habitat

Mixed-age woodlands make choice habitat for ruffs. The birds are found in a wide variety of woodland types, but they're most numerous where there are extensive stands of mixed-age aspen. The exact type of cover used depends on the bird's sex, the time of year and the region where it lives (pp. 70-75). In spring, both sexes are associated with the male's

drumming area, which has a log or other drumming platform and a dense enough canopy to protect against hawks and owls. Yet the understory should be open enough that the birds can spot ground predators and other grouse. There must be a reliable food source, such as aspen buds, nearby. The best drumming areas attract grouse year after year, even when populations are low.

After breeding, the hen leaves the drumming area to find nesting cover, which generally has less overhead cover and an open understory. Nesting hens rely on superb camouflage and lack of movement to prevent

Important Ruffed Grouse Habitats

MATURE ASPEN STANDS, preferably those consisting of male trees more than 30 years old, are prime winter feeding areas, because these trees produce the most nutritious buds. Drumming logs are often near these stands.

LOGGING ROADS offer good edge cover for grouse and a source of gravel for digestion. They also make it easy for hunters to walk into remote areas, while providing an open shooting lane.

YOUNG ASPEN STANDS, from 5 to 15 years old with some grassy openings, make good rearing areas. The aspen canopy furnishes cover from hawks and owls; the openings provide insects needed by the chicks, as well as berries.

STREAM CORRIDORS offer edge habitat combined with moist soil, an ideal combination for growing berries. The streambanks may also supply fine gravel.

being spotted by predators, and they prefer a clear view of their surroundings. The nest, a depression scratched into the ground, is usually protected on one side by a tree, stump or boulder, and is near an opening in the trees, such as a road or clear-cut. It's not unusual for mushroom hunters or others strolling the woods in spring to approach within inches of a nesting grouse before seeing it.

After the eggs hatch, the hen leads the chicks to an area with better ground cover. It could be a burned-over section of woods, a regrown clear-cut of aspen saplings or any place with new tree growth. Ideal rearing habitat has dense enough cover to conceal the chicks, but not so thick as to interfere with their feeding movements. In addition, it should have a good supply of insects, leafy green plants, fruits and berries for food. Males and hens without broods also use heavier cover in summer, usually areas of dense tree growth. They're molting at this time and would be vulnerable to predation in open areas.

When broods break up in early fall, the birds seek habitat with a good winter food source and winter cover, such as dense conifer stands. Males look for fall habitat that includes a good drumming site.

WOODED ISLANDS in cattail sloughs, lakes or rivers sometimes provide good grouse habitat. Because these areas are difficult to reach, they are ignored by the majority of hunters.

WOODLAND EDGES make prime grouse habitat, because sunlight enables brushy ground cover and food plants, such as berries, to develop.

CONIFER STANDS within hardwood forests make ideal roosting sites, especially when snow roosting is not possible. The birds can get away from ground predators, and the dense foliage hides them from hawks and owls.

ALDER THICKETS usually develop in transition zones near forest edges. Grouse use the thickets for cover and, by moving only a short distance, can find an abundance of fruit-bearing bushes.

Ruffed Grouse Hunting Basics

There are three basic elements of grouse-hunting success: identifying good grouse habitat, working it properly to flush the most birds within shooting range and making a quick, yet accurate, shot.

Specifics on where to find ruffed grouse and how to hunt them in different parts of the country will be presented in the regional discussions that follow. But regardless of where you're hunting, one rule always applies: you'll bag more ruffs by working the edges, rather than the middle, of a woods. Edges provide varied habitat, more food and better cover.

Another basic principle: your odds are generally better after the trees have lost most of their leaves than in the heavy foliage of early season. With the trees fully leaved, you're apt to hear a whir of wings and never get a glimpse of the bird.

Nevertheless, some hunters prefer early season, because the birds are still in brood groups then and have

GROUSE

not yet grown wary of hunters. You'll flush more birds, and you may be able to get closer to them than you would later in the season.

Another good time to hunt ruffs is after a fresh snow. The birds are easy to track, and you'll be able to tell if anyone else has hunted your spot.

A lone hunter generally works likely grouse habitat by walking at a fairly rapid pace, stopping for several seconds near every piece of cover likely to hold a bird. This strategy is intended to convince a hiding bird that it has been detected, and cause it to flush.

The same basic strategy can be used by two or more hunters walking in parallel. Although this method may force an individual hunter to work some less-than-ideal cover, it may also provide more shooting opportunities, because a crossing bird frequently offers a target to more than one hunter.

Pointing dogs are a vital part of grouse-hunting tradition, and a good one is a valuable asset. Close-working retrievers will also put more birds in the bag. Not only will a good dog pick up the scent of a bird in dense cover, it will help you find a higher percentage of downed birds.

Shooting grouse, which are almost always in dense cover, is much different from shooting birds in open surroundings. Normally, you don't have time to bring up your gun, swing past the bird's head and squeeze the trigger. Instead, you must learn to snap-shoot (p. 15). You instinctively calculate where the bird will be when you shoot, poke your gun barrel in that direction and pull the trigger. All of this takes only a fraction of a second. The best way to become proficient at snap-shooting is to do a lot of it. You can improve your skills by snap-shooting at clay targets.

Snap-shooting is most easily done with a light, short-barreled shotgun. Many consider the perfect grouse gun to be a 20-gauge over-and-under with improved-cylinder and modified chokes and a 24- or 26-inch barrel. The short barrel is less likely to bump limbs or catch on brush.

But some hunters argue that a 12-gauge is a better choice, especially in early season. The extra pellets in a 12-gauge load help to penetrate the thick cover. High-power shells with $7\frac{1}{2}$ shot are the best all-around load, although some prefer 6 shot in late season, when birds are flushing at longer ranges.

Because of the dense, thorny cover in which ruffed grouse are commonly found, experienced hunters wear protective eyewear and shooting gloves. Be sure to wear some blaze orange, such as a cap or vest, whenever you're in woods where there could be other hunters.

Basic Grouse-hunting Tips

LISTEN for drumming during the hunting season to pinpoint grouse. Although drumming is less frequent in fall than in spring, you'll often hear it on a quiet day.

LOOK for grouse perched in trees, epecially late in the day or in late season. Unless you spot them first, you probably won't get off a shot when they flush.

CHECK the crops of the grouse you bag. The type of food you find can provide clues on what type of cover you should be looking for.

Most southeastern ruffs are found in the Appalachians, generally at altitudes from 2,000 to 6,000 feet. Although the birds are not as plentiful as in the prime northern range, you can find plenty to hunt, if you know where to look.

Stream corridors in the foothills provide the best ruffed grouse habitat. The valleys have an abundance of shrubs, such as holly and mountain laurel, and vines, such as greenbrier, whose foliage offers food and cover in summer and fall.

Surprisingly, winter conditions in the Southeast are tougher on ruffed grouse than they are in the North. The leaves of evergreen shrubs and vines are considerably less nutritious than the buds of aspen, which is not found in this region. The birds may feed on buds of birch and dogwood, but these are also lower in nutrition.

Predation and exposure account for many grouse in winter, because of the lack of cover. Except for coniferous trees and evergreen shrubs, there is little winter foliage, and there is no snow for wintertime roosting.

Because of the strong quail-hunting tradition in this part of the country, pointing dogs, particularly English pointers and setters, are the breeds most widely used for hunting ruffs. But a wide-ranging dog is not a good choice in light cover, unless you're sure it won't "bump" (prematurely flush) the birds. Some hunters prefer a close-working flusher that does not hesitate to go into thick clumps of cover.

You can hunt ruffs in the Southeast much as you would hunt them elsewhere, but most of the hunting is done after the deer season. Hunters are reluctant to take their dogs into the woods during deer season, for safety reasons, and the woods are too thick before deer season.

Hunting Ruffed Grouse in the Southeast

With the increasing difficulty of finding places to hunt bobwhites, southeastern hunters are focusing more intently on ruffed grouse. Unlike bobwhites, ruffs abound on National Forest land, huge tracts which are open to public hunting.

Tips for Hunting Ruffs in the Southeast

LOOK for grouse along the edges of clear-cuts, where there is an abundance of brushy cover and food.

HUNT grouse around evergreen shrubs, like mountain laurel (left), in late season. The shrubs offer cover after the hardwoods lose their leaves, and some, such as holly (right), have berries that make good grouse food.

GROUSE

Hunting Ruffed Grouse in the West

In the West, where big game is king, many hunters regard ruffed grouse as nothing more than "camp meat." But this attitude means little hunting pressure and a rare opportunity for ruffed grouse enthusiasts.

Western ruffs are spooky in areas where they are commonly hunted. But in high-altitude forests or other isolated spots, they behave much the same as those in remote regions of the North. Instead of flushing when a hunter approaches, they may just hop into a nearby tree. This behavior explains why some western hunters refer to ruffs as "fool hens," a term usually reserved for blue or spruce grouse. It may also explain why many states lump all these grouse species together as "mountain grouse" for purposes of seasons and bag limits.

Like their southeastern counterparts, western ruffed grouse are closely linked to the mountains. You'll find most of the birds at altitudes of 3,500 to 8,500 feet. They're most numerous on the western slopes, which receive more rainfall than the eastern slopes and have extensive stands of mixed-growth aspen among the conifers. You'll also find ruffs along the brushy edges of logging roads and other forest openings, where berries are plentiful.

Less rainfall on the eastern slopes means fewer deciduous trees. There are pockets of birds, but they're mainly confined to creek valleys with adequate water. Look for birds in valleys dotted with small stands of aspen, along with alder and hawthorne – good sources of food and cover. Hunters who can pinpoint these key locations enjoy good grouse hunting.

A dog is not essential for western grouse hunting, but a close-working flusher, such as a springer or Labrador, helps reduce the number of birds that hop into a tree rather than fly.

Tips for Hunting Ruffs in the West

LOOK for grouse around snowberry patches. The white berries, usually found along streams and draws, are a favorite food of western grouse.

HUNT side draws and stream corridors by working up one side and down the other. The birds are not always near the bottom of the draw, so it's hard to work both sides at once.

Hunting Ruffed Grouse in the Northeast

Nowhere in the country is the grouse-hunting tradition stronger than in the Northeast. Memories of an English setter on point in a northeastern grouse woods have inspired many a classic painting.

Ruffs were once so numerous in the Northeast that orchard owners complained of damage to the buds of their apple trees. Beginning in 1870, some Massachusetts townships paid a 25-cent-per-head bounty on ruffed grouse, and, during the 1920s, the state of New Hampshire paid grouse-damage claims to many orchard owners.

But the Northeast's grouse population now faces serious long-term problems. Much of the forested land has matured to the point where shade from the heavy canopy limits growth of the ground vegetation needed for food and cover.

The dense human population in this region means hunting pressure is high and the birds, extremely wary. There is comparatively little public-hunting land, and good hunting spots are well-guarded secrets. These spots are often quite small, requiring less than an hour to cover, so you must line up several of them for a day's hunt.

Hunters in the Northeast and Great Lakes states refer to an area that consistently holds grouse as a *covert*. It could be a brushy area within an open woods, or any other small, fairly well-defined piece of grouse habitat that offers a combination of food and cover.

 GROUSE

Prime coverts often include abandoned orchards, where the new apple crop provides grouse with ample fall food; oak and beech hillsides, which furnish acorns and beechnuts; and small conifer stands, which offer roosting sites, particularly in early season, before snow roosting begins.

Be sure to work any edges that have a lot of brushy cover. Because of the small size of most coverts, edge habitat is easy to find. Common types of edge habitat include old stone fences, which also provide excellent drumming sites; roadsides; stream corridors and field margins.

Midseason hunting is usually best; trees are fully leaved in early season, and in late season, grouse hunters must compete with deer hunters.

Because hunting pressure is so heavy, grouse quickly learn the most effective escape tactics. After hunting a particular covert several times, you'll probably notice a pattern. If the birds generally flush in a certain direction, for instance, you may be able to cross them up next time by approaching from that direction, or by teaming up with other hunters to cover the most likely escape routes.

Although the tradition of hunting over an English setter is still strong in the Northeast, the spookiness of the birds and the reduced size of hunting parcels has led to an increase in popularity of close-working pointing breeds, particularly Brittany spaniels. For the same reasons, German shorthairs, springers and Labradors are gaining in popularity.

The guns and ammunition used by hunters in this region are similar to those mentioned earlier (p. 69). The cover tends to be thick and thorny, so brush pants, leather boots and shooting glasses and gloves are recommended.

Tips for Hunting Ruffs in the Northeast

HUNT along stone fences, particularly those adjacent to abandoned farm fields. Bushes and trees, such as barberry, highbush cranberry, apple and hawthorne often grow along the fences, providing an excellent food source.

LOOK for grouse around abandoned apple orchards, which are common in the Northeast. If grouse are using the area, you'll find frost-softened apples on the ground with distinct peck marks (inset).

HUNT around pine stands in cold, windy or rainy weather. The pines also offer protection from predators, such as hawks. Be ready for birds to flush from the branches instead of the ground.

CHECK topographic maps to find new grouse coverts. The maps show features like swampy areas and secondary roads leading to abandoned farmsteads not visible from the main road.

LOCATE winter concentrations of grouse by looking for snow-roosting sites. You probably won't see the birds, but you can identify places where they've been roosting if you know how to spot their exit holes (inset). In many cases, all of the grouse in a large area will concentrate in a roosting site only a few acres in size.

Hunting Ruffed Grouse in the Great Lakes Region

The abundance of prime ruffed grouse habitat in this region explains why it routinely produces the greatest grouse harvest. Extensive logging has resulted in large expanses of mixed-age aspen stands, and heavy snow cover means birds can easily escape winter storms and avoid predation by snow-roosting.

This region has huge tracts of State and National Forest land, most of which is open to public hunting. Much of this land is laced with logging roads, which provide an abundance of edge habitat and make walking easy. Roads through mixed-age clear-cuts generally offer the best hunting, because of the abundance of succulent plants, berries and brushy cover.

With so much land available for hunting, over-harvest of grouse is seldom a problem. Hunting seasons tend to be long, generally from 3 to 4 months. As in most other regions, early-season hunting is impaired by heavy foliage. And hunting gets tough in late season as birds get warier and begin to snow-roost. They may not show themselves, except during short periods when they come out to feed, usually just before sunset or on warm, sunny days.

Major grouse foods in this region include fruits and berries, such as wild grape, highbush cranberry, rose hips and cherry; and buds and catkins from aspen, birch, hazel, dogwood and hop hornbeam.

Fire-control maps, available from most State natural-resources agencies in the region, make it easy to plan your hunt. They show detailed features, such as unimproved roads, on small land parcels.

 GROUSE

Tips for Hunting Ruffs in the Great Lakes Region

APPLY a thin coat of cold-weather lubricant to the top of the barrel of a recoil-operated semi-automatic to prevent jamming in chilly weather. Make sure the barrel is free of grease before you apply the lubricant.

HUNT along trails on public land, which are common throughout the Great Lakes Region. The trails, intended for hikers, snowmobiles and all-terrain vehicles, make walking easier and provide an open shooting lane.

LOOK for ruffed grouse around vegetation that provides both food and cover. Two favorite types are hazel brush (left) and dogwood thickets (right), both of which grow in openings in the woods, or along the edges of woods and

swamps. Hazel catkins (inset) are an important grouse food, as are dogwood buds. You can identify dogwood by its whitish berries, which also make good grouse food. The berries ripen in early fall and last into winter.

In the northern part of the Great Lakes region, ideal grouse habitat consists of clear-cuts that have grown up to mixed-age aspen stands, with some mature aspen nearby for winter food. You'll also find grouse in or near alder and dogwood thickets, and in the vicinity of willow and hop hornbeam trees.

Large conifer stands abound in the northern part of the region, and grouse roost in them before there is adequate snow for roosting cover. They roost along the edges, rather than in the middle, of these stands.

In the southern part of the region, which is much more agricultural, most of the birds inhabit relatively small woodlots, often adjacent to farmsteads; wooded river-valley bluffs; and brushy corridors along streams and roadways. These birds see many more hunters and are considerably warier than those in the northern part.

In this, the heart of the ruffed grouse range, populations are considerably more cyclical (p. 65) than in the fringes of the range. Even in the "down" years, however, grouse populations are higher than in fringe areas.

Long-haired breeds, such as springer spaniels, Brittanys, English setters and wire-haired pointers are the best choice in this region, where chilly temperatures can be a problem for light-coated breeds. With all the swampy habitat, hunters should wear some type of waterproof footwear. Rubber boots are popular in warm weather; insulated, waterproof boots or felt packs are a better choice in late season.

Hunting ruffs in the Pacific Northwest is very similar to hunting them in the Great Lakes Region. The birds are found in much the same type of habitat, and hunters use comparable techniques.

SHARP-TAILED GROUSE have brown, beige and white mottling, which gives them an overall spotted appearance. The tips of the cream- to white-colored feathers on the undersides form dark brown Vs. The whitish tail has two long feathers in the center, giving it a pointed look. The long feathers are striped in males; barred in females.

Sharp-Tailed Grouse

BIOLOGY AND RANGE

Common Names: sharptail, sharpy, prairie grouse, pintail grouse, chicken, prairie chicken

Close Relatives: prairie chicken

Length: male - 17 to 19 inches
female - 16 to 18 inches

Weight: male - 2 to 2¼ pounds
female - 1¾ to 2 pounds

Clutch Size: 9 to 12

Breeding Habits: polygamous

Eating Quality: good; breast meat is dark but not particularly strong-tasting

Novice hunters often fail to shoot when sharptails flush, thinking they're hen pheasants. Although there is a definite similarity, you can easily distinguish the two by the sharptail's shorter, lighter-colored tail, its white undersides, its rocking flight and the distinctive "ducka-ducka" call it makes when it flushes. Sharptails are even more easily confused with prairie chickens, which have an overall darker coloration and a darker tail.

Primarily a resident of the Central Plains, the sharptail is found from northern Kansas through the prairie provinces of Canada and into Alaska. Their native range extended south into New Mexico, west into Washington and east into Michigan, but their range has shrunk considerably, mainly from conversion of native prairie and other grasslands to cropland and grazing land.

Although the total sharptail population has diminished in recent years, the birds are now flourishing in areas where new grasslands have been established under the Conservation Reserve Program.

Breeding habits of sharptails are much like those of prairie chickens (pp. 86-87). They establish dancing grounds, or leks, usually on high, bare ground, and the male advertises his presence with flutter jumps and cackles. He drives off subordinate males by strutting aggressively with combs swollen, head lowered and purplish gular sacs exposed. Sharptails do not produce the loud booming sound of prairie chickens; instead, they emit a lower-pitched cooing sound.

In summer, sharptails eat prairie grasses and their seeds, clover, dandelion greens and insects. In fall, they prefer green forbs and cultivated grains, especially wheat, milo, sorghum, barley, sunflowers and soybeans. They also like berries, such as blueberry, bearberry, juneberry and buffaloberry. When snow covers the ground, they survive on buds, particularly those of birch, aspen, cherry and willow.

The birds do most of their feeding early and late in the day, spending midday loafing in light cover, usually short grass. In open country they may fly several miles from feeding to roosting areas, but they normally go less than a mile.

Early in the hunting season, flocks usually number fewer than 8 birds, consisting of hens and their young. Because the young birds have never been exposed to hunting, they're easy to approach in early season. But that quickly changes, and they become extremely wary, often flushing far ahead of approaching hunters. By late season, many families combine to form large packs, which may number in the hundreds.

Winters are harsh throughout the sharptail's range, but the birds stay warm by scratching their way into a thick blanket of snow.

The meat of sharptails, including the breast, is quite dark. It has a stronger taste than that of ruffed grouse, but not strong enough for most hunters to consider it objectionable.

Short-grass prairie with brushy cover is ideal for sharptails

Sharptail Habitat

Sharptails thrive on native short-grass prairie broken by wooded stream corridors, windbreaks, cultivated fields, abandoned farmsteads and woodlots. Ideally, less than half of the area is wooded.

The grasslands provide good nesting cover, but some birds also nest in brushy areas along streams or in dried-up potholes overgrown with vegetation. The best nesting areas have some type of overhead shrub cover, such as aspen or willow, to conceal the chicks from predators.

During hunting season, sharptails feed in wheat, sunflower, alfalfa or other harvested crop fields in morning and evening. Green alfalfa fields are especially important under drought conditions. The birds also feed in patches of berries or fruit, such as rose hips, in abandoned farmsteads and along fencelines, windbreaks and stream corridors. Sharptails loaf in sparse native grasslands, CRP fields or brushy areas in midday; they're often just below a ridge, where they can see a long distance. On hot days, they seek shade under clumps of bushes. They seldom loaf in dense grass, unless they've been heavily hunted. They roost in brushy cover at night.

In winter, you'll commonly find sharptails around trees that provide good cover and buds for food. Some birds may burrow under marsh grass or high grass along fencelines and windbreaks. Conifer stands also make good winter cover, and in deep snow, most sharptails snow-roost.

When searching out sharptail-hunting areas, stay in the vicinity of traditional leks. Local farmers can be a big help in pinpointing these areas. Although some birds stray miles from leks by the time hunting season arrives, the majority stay within a mile or two.

Sharptail Hunting Techniques

Many well-traveled hunters consider sharptails one of the most challenging upland game birds. They spend much of their time in open habitat, such as stubble fields and sparse grasslands, where it's difficult to get within gun range. And they seem to grow wary of hunters earlier in the season than most other birds.

You can boost your sharptail-hunting odds by spending some time watching their daily flight patterns. If they fly to a certain field to feed in the morning, for instance, you may be able to pass-shoot them by posting along the edge of the field that evening or the next morning. If they fly into sparse prairie grass after feeding, that's the cover to hunt in midday.

When you flush a flock of early-season sharptails, watch where they land. They may not fly far, so you can follow them for a second flush. If the flock breaks up on the initial flush, the individual birds will probably hold tighter the second time. Later in the season, however, flushed birds commonly fly more than a mile, so it's not practical to follow them.

After sharptails form packs in late season, you'll rarely get close enough for a shot. If you see a pack of birds in a stubble field, for instance, try to determine where they will most likely fly when they finish feeding. If the field is bordered by grassland on one side and grain fields on the other three, the birds will probably fly into the grassland. Pass-shoot them in morning or evening by posting several hunters at 50- to 75-yard intervals along the edge of the field bordering the grassland, just as you would for prairie chickens. Or, post some hunters along this edge while others approach the birds from the opposite direction.

When planning sharptail-hunting strategy, be sure to consider the weather. The windier it is, the wilder the birds are likely to be. On very windy days, pass-shooting may be your best option; otherwise, you won't be able to get close enough for a shot. In hot weather, the birds tend to sit tight, often in the shade of dense bushes. On calm, quiet mornings, listen for sharptails "talking." Their chuckles and whines sound somewhat like those of barnyard chickens.

Wide-ranging pointers are the best choice for early-season sharptails. The birds hold tight then, and these big runners can cover a lot of ground quickly. When the birds get skittish later in the season, you'll do better with a close worker, like a Labrador, golden retriever or Brittany.

A 12-gauge semi-automatic or pump shotgun is recommended for sharptail hunting, because multiple bird flushes are quite common. Most hunters use a modified choke and high-power size 6 or $7\frac{1}{2}$ shot in early season; a full choke and size 4 shot in late season.

Sharptail hunting requires no special equipment, although a comfortable pair of lightweight boots is a good idea for long-distance walking. Lip balm will prevent split lips caused by the relentless high winds in the plains country.

Tips for Finding and Hunting Sharptails

SCOUT for sharptails "budding" in trees early in the day. This way, you know the area holds birds, and you can hunt surrounding grasslands after they finish feeding.

HUNT sharptails around berry patches on hot, sunny days in early season. The patches provide an ideal combination of food and shade.

LOOK for sharptails in standing sunflower fields after the heads are dry and dropping seeds. You'll also find the birds in cut sunflowers. Normally, they'll be within 50 yards of the field edges.

WORK the lee sides of hills on windy days. Not only will you find the most birds there, shooting is easier because the birds can't flush with the wind.

CHECK shelterbelts between crop fields to find roosting sharptails. These areas are best in early morning and in midday.

GROUSE

Blue Grouse

BLUE GROUSE males are dark blue-gray over most of the upper body, with some brown and black on the wings and undersides. The combs and gular sacs vary from red to yellow. The tail is black and may have a light gray band at the end. Females (inset) are considerably smaller and have an overall brownish coloration, with more noticeable mottling on the wings and neck, and a brownish gray tail, which may also have a light gray band.

BIOLOGY AND RANGE

Common Names: dusky grouse, sooty grouse, fool hen, mountain grouse, hooter, pine grouse, Richardson's grouse
Close Relatives: ruffed, spruce and sage grouse
Length: male - 19 to 23 inches
  female - 17 to 20 inches
Weight: male - 2½ to 3 pounds
  female - 1½ to 2 pounds
Clutch Size: 6 to 9
Breeding Habits: polygamous
Eating Quality: excellent; white breast meat similar to that of ruffed grouse, but breast is much larger

Springtime hikers in mountainous areas of the West are often puzzled by muffled owl-like hooting sounds remindful of nothing else in nature. The sounds, emitted by male blue grouse during the breeding season, explain why the birds are commonly referred to as "hooters," and their breeding areas as "hooting grounds."

Males hoot to attract females and announce their territorial claim to other males. While hooting, they strut about with their tails fanned, combs swollen and gular sacs inflated. They aggressively charge other males that attempt to invade their territory, often making physical contact.

Although blue grouse are the second-largest member of the grouse family, few people ever see them, because of the remote habitat they occupy. They spend most of the year, including winter, at altitudes from 8,000 to 12,000 feet, using dense conifer stands for cover and food. Their ability to eat needles, twigs and seeds of conifers, particularly Douglas fir, allows them to stay at high elevations despite the heavy snow cover.

Late in the winter, the birds begin moving to lower altitudes, where there are more openings in the conifers, for breeding. They use valleys as downhill and uphill migration routes.

Males return to the high country, usually the vicinity of the treeline, soon after breeding. Females move into still lower valleys, where there is more food and ground cover, to nest and raise their broods. These valleys produce the earliest crop of berries and insects, which make excellent food for the chicks. As these foods become available at

 GROUSE

higher altitudes, females and their young begin to move up.

Although many brood groups begin working their way up the mountain even before the season opens, some remain at lower altitudes through the first week or two of the season. Look for birds on ridge tops and slopes above the valleys, particularly around aspen stands with a dense understory, or in semiopen stands of conifers. By late season, nearly all the birds are at high altitudes, where it's much more difficult for hunters to reach them.

If you're not sure what altitude the birds are at, try driving some logging roads early or late in the day, looking for birds roosting in trees. When you spot a bird or two, it's a good bet there will be many more at the same altitude.

Once you determine the right altitude range, look for patches of conifers or openings in the conifers on high ridges; the birds do not like dense cover. A single hunter should work the edges of the openings, particularly around blackberry, blueberry or juneberry patches. A group of hunters should spread out at 50-yard intervals and walk parallel at the same approximate altitude.

Don't start your hunt too early in the morning; the birds will still be roosting in trees, and you'll walk right past them. Most birds will be on the ground by midmorning. But even then, they may refuse to flush, especially if they haven't been hunted much.

Close-working flushers, such as Labradors or springers, will put these birds in the air. Pointers will find the birds, but in some cases, birds will hop into a tree when the dog goes on point.

A lightweight shotgun, 12- to 20-gauge, is recommended for long treks in steep terrain. A modified choke, or a modified/improved-cylinder in a double-barrel, is a good all-around choice. Use high-power shells with size 6 to 7½ shot.

Tips for Finding and Hunting Blue Grouse

LOOK for blues around isolated patches of mature conifers, especially those near the top of grassy hillsides and ridges.

CHECK berry patches bordering meadows, particularly after the first freeze, which increases the berries' sugar content.

HUNT blues in wooded draws coursing through open grasslands. Slopes that are completely wooded hold fewer birds.

LOCATE good blue grouse areas by watching for the birds in trees. Their large size makes them easy to spot at a distance.

WORK draws connected on both ends by a switchback road. Have someone drop you off at the top and pick you up at the bottom.

GROUSE

SAGE GROUSE are grayish brown with dark brown, black and cream-colored mottling above. In flight, the dark belly contrasts with the light undersides of the wings. Cocks have long, pointed tail feathers that fan out when they strut, a whitish breast and a black throat and belly. Hens (inset) have a smaller black belly and their color is more uniform

GROUSE

Sage Grouse

In terms of sheer size, sage grouse are king of the upland game birds. Sometimes called "bombers" because of their size, cocks may weigh 7 pounds or more. Hens are noticeably smaller, weighing up to 4 pounds. These huge birds once flourished throughout the semiarid plains country in mountainous regions of the West.

As their name suggests, the birds rely heavily on sagebrush for food and cover. But as more and more sage is cleared to make cropland or grazing land, their range has shrunk considerably. They're now found mainly in Wyoming, Montana, Idaho, Utah and Nevada.

Sage grouse eat sage buds, leaves and shoots throughout the year, but rely on sage most heavily in winter. They occasionally eat grasses, alfalfa, berries, small grains and insects.

The birds do most of their feeding early and late in the day and spend the middle of the day loafing in gullies and draws. They're often found near water, especially in hot, dry weather. The best habitat has a creek or water hole within a half mile of the feeding area.

Sage grouse rely heavily on their eyesight to spot predators. This explains why they're often seen standing alert and stretching their neck. They usually run off and hide to escape danger, but will flush out of range when heavily hunted.

The availability of sage dictates the birds' seasonal movement patterns. When snow covers sagebrush at high elevations, they often move to lower elevations, where there is less snow, or to high, wind-swept ridges. They may go as far as 20 miles.

Like sharptails and prairie chickens, sage grouse have an elaborate communal mating ritual. In spring, groups of 100 or more gather on the breeding grounds, where the cocks strut, fan their tail and inflate the huge gular sacs on the front of their neck to establish dominance. The few cocks that prove to be dominant breed with most of the hens.

Hens often nest beneath sage plants, scratching a large depression into the ground. After the eggs hatch, the hen stays with the brood, which usually numbers from four to six chicks, through the summer and into the early part of the hunting season. Often, two to four hens and their broods flock together at this time. Hens without broods and cocks form separate groups numbering three to six birds. Late in the season, many hens and their broods join to form flocks that sometimes include more than 100 birds.

Sage grouse undergo population cycles about 10 years in length, much like those of ruffed grouse. Just as ruffed grouse cycles possibly relate to cycles of snowshoe hares (p. 65), sage grouse cycles may relate to those of jackrabbits.

BIOLOGY AND RANGE

Common Names: sage hen, sage turkey, sage cock, sage chicken

Close Relatives: blue, ruffed and spruce grouse

Length: male - 26 to 30 inches
female - 20 to 24 inches

Weight: male - 5 to 7 pounds
female - 3 to 4 pounds

Clutch Size: 6 to 9

Breeding Habits: polygamous

Eating Quality: young birds, excellent; older ones may have strong, sagey flavor depending on bird's age (p. 85)

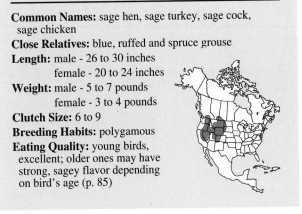

The very best sage is near cropfields or water

Sage Grouse Habitat

Gently sloping, open country with large sagebrush flats and few trees makes the best sage grouse habitat. Summers are usually hot and rainfall low. The birds avoid sagebrush that is too dense or too high, because it impairs their vision. They may be found at altitudes up to 9,000 feet.

When the ground is snow-covered, the birds seem drawn to specific patches of sage, probably because it is higher in nutritional value than other sage.

Because of the great expanses of sagebrush habitat, a little inside information on bird populations can save you a lot of futile walking. It pays to check with field offices of local wildlife agencies to get current information on bird counts. As a rule, the best sage grouse areas change very little from year to year. Once you find a good spot, it should continue to produce as long as the quality of the habitat holds up.

Concentrate your efforts on sagebrush flats, water holes and stream corridors early and late in the day, when air temperatures are cooler. If you want to hunt in the midday heat, work draws with water and heavier sage.

The basic hunting technique is simple: find the right kind of sagebrush, and walk into the wind. If you're hunting in a party, stay 30 to 50 yards away from adjacent hunters. Sage grouse tend to flush wild if a dog pushes them, so close workers, such as Brittanys and Labradors, are most popular. A wide-ranging pointing dog can help you locate birds on large sagebrush flats, but it must be trained to hold a firm point at the first scent of a bird.

You can also hunt sage grouse much the same way you would hunt antelope. Simply drive the back roads, using binoculars to spot some birds; then plan a stalk that will bring you within shooting distance. Be quiet and keep a low profile when approaching the birds, however, or they will probably flush out of range.

When sage grouse flush, they fly slowly and laboriously at first, but can reach speeds of 40 mph or more with a tail wind. But their size makes it appear that they're flying much more slowly, so if you're missing too many shots, try exaggerating your lead (opposite).

The birds often rise in small groups, rather than one tight covey. Be prepared for late flushers, and walk the area again for any tight sitters. Sometimes they'll sneak off to the side as much as 100 yards.

Be sure to precisely mark the spot where the birds land. Normally they won't go much farther than a quarter-mile. Like Hungarian partridge, the flock usually stays together and can be flushed several times, assuming they land in cover thick enough to hold them and you get there in a hurry. Otherwise, they'll run.

Like most other upland game birds, sage grouse become much spookier as the hunting season progresses. If they've been heavily hunted, you'll find it nearly impossible to get within shotgun range by season's end. And when the birds flush, they often fly out of sight.

Rainy weather upsets the normal hunting pattern, because the birds do not like to stay in wet sagebrush. Instead, they move into open areas, such as rocky outcrops, where they are hard to approach.

In early season, a 12- to 20-gauge shotgun with a modified choke and high-power shells with size 6 shot are good choices for sage grouse. Later, a full choke and size 4 shot work better.

The eating quality of sage grouse varies from poor to excellent, depending on the age and sex of the bird. Adult males tend to be tough and have a strong, sage flavor, as do some adult hens. But young birds have a taste and texture similar to that of pheasant. Experienced sage grouse hunters shoot only young birds or hens, which are easy to distinguish from cocks.

EXAGGERATE your lead when shooting at sage grouse. Because the birds are so large, they appear to be flying slowly, so the tendency is to shoot behind them.

Tips for Hunting Sage Grouse

MARK the spot where you dropped a bird by tying a piece of biodegradable ribbon to a piece of sage. Birds are easy to lose in the sea of sage, and the ribbon gives you a reference so you can return to your starting point.

WORK the areas around water holes to find sage grouse, especially during dry spells. Normally, you'll find the birds within one-half mile of the water.

HUNT sage adjacent to crop fields, where they are available. The birds feed in the crop fields early and late in the day, and loaf in the sage in midday.

GROUSE

85

PRAIRIE CHICKENS have dark brown or black barring on a beige background. The chin and undersides are lighter beige. Males (main photo) have long pinnae, large gular sacs, a prominent yellow comb above the eye and short tail bars that extend only across the central feathers.

Females (top inset) have barely noticeable pinnae and bars that extend completely across the tail. Lesser prairie chickens are slightly smaller, and the males have shorter pinnae than those of male greaters (bottom inset). They also make a softer booming noise and utter a gobbling sound.

Prairie Chicken

The long neck feathers, or *pinnae*, of the male prairie chicken explain the official species name: pinnated grouse. When erect, the pinnae resemble horns jutting above the head.

Prairie chickens once flourished throughout the vast native grasslands of the central United States and south-central Canada. Their populations were bolstered by the introduction of small grains, but as more and more grassland fell to the plow, their numbers diminished greatly. Surprisingly, the birds' range has expanded to the north, where small-grain crops provide a good winter food source. They have been reintroduced into Wisconsin, North Dakota, Oklahoma and Saskatchewan.

There are three prairie chicken varieties: greater, lesser and Attwater. The greater prairie chicken, by far the most numerous, inhabits tall-grass prairie in the northern part of the range; the lesser, short-grass, semidesert prairie in the southwestern part. There is

presently no open season for the Attwater. Found only along the Texas Gulf Coast, it is classified as an endangered species. Only six states now have prairie chicken seasons, with Kansas heading the list in terms of number harvested.

The prairie chicken is known for its spectacular courtship ritual. Adult males attract females by dancing and strutting with head down, wings lowered, pinnae erect and gular sacs inflated. They often jump

BIOLOGY AND RANGE

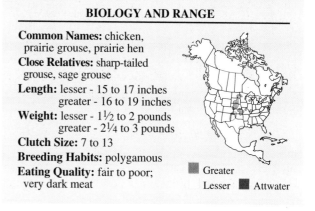

Common Names: chicken, prairie grouse, prairie hen

Close Relatives: sharp-tailed grouse, sage grouse

Length: lesser - 15 to 17 inches
greater - 16 to 19 inches

Weight: lesser - 1½ to 2 pounds
greater - 2¼ to 3 pounds

Clutch Size: 7 to 13

Breeding Habits: polygamous

Eating Quality: fair to poor; very dark meat

Greater

Lesser   Attwater

and cackle with wings fluttering. The large gular sacs serve as resonators, boosting the volume of their mating call to make a booming sound that can be heard for up to a mile. This explains why their courtship areas, or leks, are also called "booming grounds."

Important fall and winter prairie chicken foods include small grains, such as wheat, soybeans, milo, sorghum and sometimes corn. The birds also feed in cut-alfalfa and winter-wheat fields, and eat a variety of seeds and leaves of prairie plants. In winter, when these foods are not available, they feed on the buds of birch or elm.

Prairie chickens are strong flyers, sometimes traveling several miles from the grass fields where they roost to their feeding grounds. They normally fly out to feed from just before to just after sunrise. They return to the grass fields after feeding, then fly out to feed again an hour or two before sunset. Prairie chickens avoid areas with trees, such as creek bottoms, that draw many other kinds of upland birds.

In early season, some hunters comb the prairie with big-running pointers to find single chickens and family groups. This is mainly an early-season, still-weather option, because that's the only time the birds will hold tight. Nevertheless, hunting may be tough, because of the large expanses of prairie involved.

Once prairie chickens have been hunted a few times, they usually flush out of gun range. If you see a bird flush wild, run toward the spot where it got up; you might find more. There's usually no point in trying to follow birds that flush wild; they may fly for miles.

Pass-shooting is by far the best technique in mid- to late season, after the birds get spooky. As the weather gets colder, flock size increases and birds tend to feed more heavily in the crop fields. By late season, flocks may number from 50 to 200 birds.

The secret to successful pass-shooting is to find the fields prairie chickens are using, then hunt between roosting and feeding areas. Set up a blind, or just hide in a clump of brush along a fenceline. Start hunting early; the birds may fly in before sunrise. Pass-shooting is better on calm, sunny days than on windy, foggy or rainy days.

Pass-shooting prairie chickens is much like pass-shooting ducks. The birds are tough to hit, because they're moving faster than you think. Using the sustained-lead technique (p. 15), experiment with leads ranging from 3 to 10 feet.

A 12- to 20-gauge, improved-cylinder- or modified-choke shotgun and high-power shells with $7\frac{1}{2}$ shot are good choices in early season; later, you may want to switch to a full choke and 6 shot. For pass-shooting, use a gun with a 28- to 30-inch barrel.

Tips for Hunting Prairie Chickens

SCOUT potential feeding fields to determine the birds' movement patterns; then set up your blind (below) accordingly.

MAKE a blind out of a 4x4 piece of plywood; set it along the feeding-field side of a fence. Look for birds flying in low over the grass field; they nearly always fly in from the same direction.

RUSH to a point when hunting prairie chickens with dogs. Even in early season, they may not hold long enough for a shot if you're too slow. Later in the season, the birds are even less likely to hold.

Spruce Grouse

SPRUCE GROUSE males have an overall grayish black coloration, with a black throat, cinnamon-tipped tail, red combs, and white-tipped feathers from the lower throat down the undersides. Females (inset) have a brownish gray, mottled back with lighter vermiculations, and beige undersides with darker brown barring.

When hunters talk about spruce grouse, the terms "sluice," "Arkansas" or "ground swat" are apt to come up in the conversation. The bird's inclination to sit tight rather than flush accounts for its reputation as one of the least intelligent game birds and most deserving of the moniker: fool hen.

The birds' moronic behavior is most obvious in remote areas where they seldom see hunters. If they're hunted regularly, however, they can offer a shooting challenge.

BIOLOGY AND RANGE

Common Names: fool hen, spruce partridge, Franklin grouse, Canada grouse, swamp grouse, black partridge

Close Relatives: ruffed and blue grouse

Length: male - 16 to 17 inches
female - 15 to 16 inches

Weight: male - 1¼ pounds
female - 1 pound

Clutch Size: 5 to 9

Breeding Habits: polygamous

Eating Quality: fair; meat may have strong taste because of conifer-needle diet

GROUSE

Found mainly in the northern states, most of Canada and mountainous areas of the West, spruce grouse are birds of climax coniferous forests sprinkled with a few deciduous trees, primarily alder, aspen and birch. The conifers furnish good roosting sites for spruce grouse, and their needles make good winter food. Openings in the forest provide grassy cover for brood raising and a source of berries, particularly blueberry and cranberry.

The best spruce grouse habitat has a fairly open understory with roadways or streambeds to provide the gravel needed for digestion. Often, you'll find the birds around edges of bogs or swamps.

Spruce grouse populations are much less cyclical than those of ruffed grouse. Their survival rate is considerably higher, meaning that the population consists of a larger percentage of adult birds. In most parts of their range, numbers are holding up well, unless there has been extensive logging.

Assuming the foliage is not too dense, hunting is best in early season. Once snow covers the ground, the birds spend most of their time perched in trees, where they're almost impossible to locate or flush.

Because spruce grouse are apt to sit tight, a hunter without a dog may walk past a lot of them, even if he uses the walk-and-pause technique. A close-working flusher, such as a golden retriever or Labrador, will root those birds out of the cover. Any dog that ranges too far, however, will push birds into the trees before you get there. Pointers may pin birds down, but you might have trouble flushing them.

The guns and ammunition used for spruce grouse are identical to those used for ruffed grouse (p. 69), and the same snap-shooting skills are required. No special equipment is needed, with the exception of rubber boots if you'll be hunting in boggy areas.

Tips for Finding and Hunting Spruce Grouse

CHECK openings in the conifers to find spruce grouse. The openings offer edge habitat in the otherwise dense forest.

HUNT spruce grouse along gravel roads through conifer forests. The birds find needed grit along the roads, and the clearing offers an open shooting lane.

LOOK for spruce grouse along stream edges, which often produce a bountiful crop of berries. Like gravel roads, the streams also provide grit.

WHITE-TAILED PTARMIGAN in summer plumage have black, buff and white mottling on the back and rump. Their outer tail feathers are white, as opposed to black in other summer-phase ptarmigan. Winter-phase birds (inset) are all white, except for the eyes and bill. The birds weigh about ¾ pound and are 12 to 13 inches long.

Ptarmigan

Known for their chameleonlike qualities, ptarmigan are more a curiosity than an important sport-hunting bird. Their color changes from nearly pure white in winter to various shades of brown in summer, enabling them to blend in perfectly with their surroundings.

Ptarmigan (pronounced 'tar-mi-gan) are found mainly on barren tundra, where they're commonly shot for food by native Americans. Of the three species, the only one whose range extends into the lower 48 states is the white-tailed ptarmigan, the smallest member of the grouse family. It is found only in high mountains of the West. Ptarmigan differ from other

grouse species in that they have hairlike feathers on their toes, an adaptation to the frigid climate.

Another ptarmigan curiosity: during the winter, they form sexually segregated flocks that may number in the thousands. Male flocks prefer alpine habitat; female flocks, lower altitude, with more sheltered areas. Unlike other grouse species, ptarmigan are monogamous, meaning the male breeds with only a single female.

If you're interested in hunting these unique birds and are planning a Canadian or Alaskan big-game hunt in ptarmigan country, ask your outfitter to set up a day or two of ptarmigan hunting. Bring along a 12- to 20-gauge shotgun with an improved-cylinder choke and field loads with 7½ shot.

GROUSE

WILLOW PTARMIGAN in summer plumage have heavy, dark brown barring on the back, black outer tail feathers and a chestnut-brown head. Winter-phase willow ptarmigan (inset) are all white, except for the black tail feathers, and do not have a black eye streak. The birds weigh 1¼ to 1½ pounds and are 15 to 17 inches long.

ROCK PTARMIGAN in winter plumage are almost completely white, with a black streak on either side of the eye and black outer tail feathers that stay black all year. Summer-phase rock ptarmigan (inset) are grayer than willow ptarmigan, without the chestnut-brown head. The birds weigh just over a pound and are 12 to 14 inches long.

Quail

These tiny game birds generally weigh less than 8 ounces, and even the largest are no more than a foot long. But what they lack in size, they make up for in sporting quality. Millions of hunters consider them the ultimate wingshot challenge.

Besides the well-known bobwhite and California quail, and the lesser-known mountain quail, this family consists of three species of "desert quail," including the Gambel's, scaled and Mearns quail. As their name suggests, desert quail are found mainly in the desert Southwest.

Quail rank only behind doves in terms of total number taken per year. Bobwhites make up by far the highest percentage of the harvest; Mearns, the lowest.

Highly gregarious, quail are almost always found in coveys. This behavior, which probably evolved as a defense against predators, is also an effective defense against hunters. Not only do sentries give the covey advance warning of a hunter's approach, hunters often hurry their shots too much in the excitement of a covey flush.

Some species of quail, such as Gambel's and scaled, form large wintering groups that may number more than 100 birds. Other species form smaller late-season groups consisting of two or more coveys. Although these big groups are not as wild as a grouse pack (p. 62), they tend to be spookier than the smaller, early-season coveys.

Quail are easy to recognize, not only because of their small size and covey behavior, but also their short, stout bill. Many species have a distinctive plume or crest on the head. Unlike grouse, their lower legs are not feathered.

All quail are monogamous. They do not perform the elaborate mating rituals typical of the grouse, nor are they as territorial. Quail seldom produce more than one brood per year, but if a brood is lost to predators or bad weather, they usually renest.

BOBWHITES have a mottled brownish back and wings. Cocks (right) have a white throat, a white stripe extending across the forehead to the base of the neck and whitish undersides with brown and black specks. Hens (left) have a buff-colored throat and forehead stripe and the background color of the undersides is beige.

Bobwhite Quail

If you've experienced the thrill of a bobwhite covey exploding at your feet, you should have no trouble understanding why this diminutive game bird is so popular. In the excitement of the flush, many a novice empties his gun long before the birds reach the proper shooting range, and the covey flies away untouched.

Bobwhites are found over a much larger range than other quail species. They're more tolerant of cold weather, yet they also thrive in hot, semiarid climates, assuming they can find a permanent water source. In the southwestern part of their range, bobwhite populations are highly dependent on spring rainfall, as are populations of most desert quail.

Another reason bobwhites flourish over such a large area is their ability to use a wide variety of foods – more than 600, according to one food-habit study.

BIOLOGY AND RANGE

Common Names: bobs, partridge, quail, American colin
Close Relatives: Gambel's quail, California quail, scaled quail
Length: 9 to 10 inches
Weight: 6 to 8 ounces
Clutch Size: 12 to 16
Breeding Habits: monogamous
Eating Quality: excellent

Typical bobwhite roosting ring

Seeds of grasses, weeds and legumes are the main-stays of the birds' diet, but they also eat the greens of these plants, along with acorns, pine seeds, insects, berries and cultivated crops, such as corn, wheat, milo and soybeans.

The distinctive mating call of the cock, "bob-bob-white," is commonly heard in spring. After he attracts a mate, he scratches a shallow depression in the ground, usually in grassy or brushy cover. He uses grass to line the nest and make a dome over at least one side of it. The hen incubates the eggs, which are subject to heavy predation, especially by skunks and snakes. Sometimes, two or three attempts are needed to bring off a brood, with clutch size decreasing on each successive attempt.

The chicks, along with the hen, leave the nest within a few hours of hatching, but don't go far. Normally, they spend their entire life in an area of 40 acres or less, seldom venturing more than 50 yards from the edge of cover.

Bobwhites feed in grassy fields or harvested crop fields early and late in the day. They may feed later on cold or wet mornings, and if hunting pressure is heavy, the feeding periods tend to be shorter. After feeding, they pick up grit before returning to adjacent heavy cover, such as woodlots, wooded creek bottoms and brushy fencelines, draws and ditches. The thicker and more secluded the cover is, the more likely it will hold birds.

In the southwestern part of their range, the key to finding bobwhites is water, particularly in a dry year. Rather than combing dry, windblown plains for a few birds, confine your efforts to brushy stream corridors, grassy fringes of water holes and areas around man-made watering devices, called *guzzlers*.

A covey, which usually consists of 10 to 15 birds, often forms a *roosting ring* (above), with tails point-ed toward the center and heads facing outward. In this position, the birds conserve body heat and easily spot any approaching predators.

Bobwhites are ideal quarry for the wingshot. When faced with danger, the birds tend to freeze rather than run, so you have time to get into position for a close shot. When they flush, they usually fly in different directions, a tactic that confuses hunters. But they usually fly no more than 200 yards, unless they've been heavily hunted.

After the covey breaks up, individual birds emit a rallying call, "whoo-ee-whoo," to notify other covey members of their whereabouts.

Once you find a covey, chances are it will stay in the same vicinity all season. And there will most likely be another covey in the same area next year, because it offers the right habitat mix.

The size of the annual bobwhite crop depends main-ly on weather. In the North, many birds die of starva-tion or freeze to death in severe winters with deep snow. In much of the bobwhite's range, heavy spring rains wash out their nests, but in arid regions, rain means abundant food and high populations.

Although the bobwhite is by far the most common and widespread North American quail species, its range and abundance have shrunk in recent years due to loss of habitat. The decrease in the number of small family farms and the trend toward "clean farming" have meant a severe reduction in the habitat diversity needed for bobwhites to prosper.

The decline has been most noticeable in the South-east, where the quail-hunting tradition is strongest. You may get some good shooting on public hunting lands, but such areas are in short supply and burn out early in the season. Private lands with good numbers of quail are usually reserved for friends and family. Although many plantations have excellent bobwhite populations, hunts can be expensive and too arranged for the tastes of many hunters.

If you don't have connections, your chances of finding a good quail-hunting spot are better in the northern reaches of the range. Public hunting land is more plen-tiful there, and the birds are not in such great demand.

PINE STANDS that have been thinned out to allow sunlight penetration are common throughout the southeastern states. They have a grassy understory that is ideal for bob-

whites. The understory must be burned every few years to maintain desirable seed plants and to improve visibility for shooting.

HARVESTED CROP FIELDS attract quail that feed on the crop residue. The best fields have good cover along the edge, enabling quail to quickly hide from predators.

FOOD PLOTS, planted by private landowners and conservation agencies, provide fall and winter food as well as brood habitat in summer.

WATER HOLES draw quail in arid regions. Although quail can live on water from their food, the area around a water hole has higher bird numbers.

BRUSH PILES, intentionally placed for quail cover, have bolstered bobwhite populations in areas that lack sufficient woody loafing cover.

BRUSHY FENCEROWS may be the only remaining quail cover in many agricultural areas. The best fence-rows have trees, such as osage orange, with low-growing or spiny branches that help keep out predators and prevent cattle from grazing underneath. This way, grasses can grow there, offering quail good roosting and escape cover.

GRASSY EDGES of crop fields, or grass patches within them, provide roosting cover adjacent to feeding areas.

BRUSHY DRAWS, ditches and creek beds are important habitat types throughout the bobwhite's range. They furnish good roosting and escape cover.

PLUM THICKETS, or other types of impenetrable brush clumps, are classic bobwhite hiding spots. The same clump may hold a covey year after year.

ABANDONED FARMSTEADS, especially those with tree groves and tall weeds, offer good bobwhite roosting and escape cover plus refuge from winter storms.

Techniques for Hunting Bobwhites

On a traditional southern quail hunt, hunters ride in a horse- or mule-drawn wagon or on horseback to follow wide-ranging pointing dogs. When the dogs pin down a covey, the hunters leisurely walk in for a shot.

Although hunting from a "quail wagon" is becoming more and more of a rarity, most experienced quail hunters regard pointing dogs as an indispensable tool. The classic quail dog is a big runner, such as an English pointer or a southern-bred English setter, but closer-working dogs, like Gordon setters and Brittanys, may work better in heavy cover. And some hunters prefer flushing dogs for penetrating dense tangles of brush.

The usual technique is to let the dog quarter ahead of the hunters, often several hundred yards ahead. If you're using a retriever along with a pointing dog, be sure to keep the retriever at heel so it doesn't flush the birds prematurely.

When the dog goes on point, the hunters walk in to flush the birds, approaching at the same angle the dog is pointing. This boosts the odds of the birds flushing straight away, offering the easiest possible shot.

Try to stay calm and pick out the most obvious bird in the covey. If you flock-shoot, you'll be lucky to connect; there's a lot more "air" between the birds than it seems. Be sure to reload quickly after shooting; a straggler or two may flush later.

After the flush, keep your eye on the singles. The scent tends to "wash off" when the birds fly, making it hard for dogs to find them. Your odds will improve if you mark the birds carefully, then wait for 15 minutes or so before going after them, giving them time to begin calling and spread fresh scent. In areas with plenty of birds, most hunters opt to look for new coveys, rather than pursue singles.

Estimating shooting range is a big problem for novice quail hunters. Because of the bird's small size, they seem farther away than they really are. The tendency is to begin shooting before the birds get into range, and stop before they're out of range.

Mark downed birds carefully. The minimal scent emitted by downed birds makes retrieves difficult for a dog. And a bird that is still alive will hunker down and compress its feathers, further reducing the amount of scent it emits.

If you don't have a dog, you can still bag some quail by walking brushy fencelines, draws and ditches, stopping at every likely looking clump of cover. You may have to wait a minute or so to make the birds nervous enough to flush.

Bobwhites are often hard to find at the beginning of the season, because most of the crops and grasses are still standing. And by late season, the birds become spooky, often running ahead of hunters and flushing out of range. The best hunting is normally in mid-season, after most of the crops have been harvested, but before the birds get too spooky.

Late-season hunters commonly make the mistake of going out too early in the day, especially in cold weather. Bobwhites usually wait until well after sunrise before moving to their feeding areas. But early-morning hunting often pays off at the beginning of the season.

The classic bobwhite gun is a 20-gauge over-and-under or side-by-side with improved-cylinder and modified chokes and barrels no more than 26 inches long. Field loads with 8 shot are a good all-around choice. In early season, however, some hunters prefer a skeet choke and 9 shot; in late season, a modified choke and $7\frac{1}{2}$ shot.

Snakes can be a problem in the South, especially in early season. If you're hunting in known snake country, be sure to wear tall, snakeproof boots or chaps and carry a snakebite kit. In the Southwest, you may wish to outfit your dog with boots (p. 103) to protect its paws from cactus spines.

HUNT into the wind whenever possible. Allow the dog to range widely, covering a lot of ground to air-scent birds and investigate likely cover.

ALLOW your dog to range one to two hundred yards ahead when hunting with the wind at your back. Then direct it to hunt back toward you, into the wind. Any birds it points will be pinned between you and the dog.

WATCH the dog closely for a point. If the dog has been trained in good *bird manners*, you don't have to hurry to the spot. It will hold the birds for as long as it takes you to get there.

WALK past the point to flush the birds, while the dog remains *steady to wing*. If you allow the dog to flush them, you're encouraging poor bird manners, and a dog chasing low-flying birds could be shot by mistake.

LOCATE downed birds by checking any spot where the dog is *pointing dead*. Some pointing dogs are natural retrievers, but if the dog is not so inclined, don't encourage it. Forced retrieves also lead to poor bird manners.

TRAIN your dog to *honor the point* of another dog by freezing well behind it. This way, the second dog won't "steal the point" of the first or bump the birds.

Tips for Hunting Bobwhites

SEND your hunting partners around both sides of a thicket when your dog goes on point. This way, someone is sure to get a clear shot when the birds flush.

WORK any brushy corners of fencelines. Corners tend to have heavier vegetation, because farm machinery cannot get into them.

LEARN to "read" your pointing dog to get a better idea of the covey's location. If the dog is pointing with its head high (left), the covey could be as much as 10 yards upwind. But if its head is low (right), the covey could be very close. Each dog reacts a little differently, however, so you must learn to read your own dog.

KEEP your eyes on the spot where a bird was downed, and direct another hunter to it. This helps recover birds in large-cover parcels.

MOVE IN with your partner to flush a covey. This way, you'll both be in good position for a shot, and nobody will be in the line of fire.

TRAMP the cover thoroughly to flush a single. It may hold tight until you practically step on it.

POST one hunter near a likely escape route, such as an opening in the trees, before flushing the birds. They avoid flying into dense cover.

GAMBEL'S QUAIL have a black, teardrop-shaped plume like that of California quail (p. 104), but no scale pattern on the abdomen. The upper body is grayish brown to brown; the undersides, buff-colored. Males have a rusty crown and a black forehead, throat and abdomen. Females (inset) have a smaller plume and no black throat or abdomen, but may have brown streaks on the undersides.

Gambel's Quail

Normally found in areas that receive less than 10 inches of annual precipitation, Gambel's quail are even more tolerant of hot, dry conditions than the other types of desert quail (p. 93). But they cannot cope with cold weather as well as other quail species.

Even though the birds can survive dry conditions, populations are highest in years of heavy winter and spring rains. Populations tend to be more stable near the bases of desert mountains, because rainfall in these areas is more consistent. Rain fuels the early spring green-up needed to provide the nutrients hens require to lay big clutches.

The desert habitat favored by Gambel's quail has a mix of weeds, grasses and brush, such as mesquite,

Apache plume, catclaw, hackberry, creosote and saltbush. Quail feed in the cool, dewy weeds and grasses early and late in the day, and spend midday loafing in brushy cover. The brush is taller and denser than that used by scaled quail (p. 111), and also provides cover for nighttime roosting.

Typical Gambel's quail habitat

Prickly pear cactus is important in cattle country, because cows won't graze on the grass beneath it. Heavily grazed areas generally lack sufficient ground cover and support few birds.

Gambel's quail eat a wide variety of weed and grass seeds; the leaves, flowers and seeds of legumes, such as alfalfa and clover; mesquite beans; juniper berries and the fruit of prickly pear. Although they can survive on water they get from their food, they thrive in areas with a permanent water source, such as a stock tank, stream or guzzler.

The birds have a well-deserved reputation for being runners, especially on the "desert pavement." In good cover, however, they'll hold surprisingly tight. This explains why experienced Gambel's quail hunters confine their efforts to areas with plenty of grassy and brushy cover.

Coveys usually consist of 10 to 40 birds but, by late fall, can number more than 100. Coveys often group more loosely than those of other quail and may not flush in unison.

BIOLOGY AND RANGE

Common Names: desert quail, Arizona quail
Close Relatives: California quail, mountain quail, scaled quail
Length: 9 to 11 inches
Weight: 5½ to 6½ ounces
Clutch size: 9 to 15
Breeding Habits: monogamous
Eating Quality: excellent; breast meat is white and tender

One of the best ways to hunt Gambel's quail is to walk the slopes of *arroyos*, gullies carved by moving water. Work the sides of the slopes early and late in the day, when the birds are most active. The lower, brushier areas are more productive in midday, when the birds are looking for shade. The best arroyos generally hold a little water.

Most Gambel's quail hunters prefer pointing dogs over flushers, although close-working flushers are a good choice in thick cover. Because of the hot climate, many hunters use short-haired pointing breeds, such as German shorthairs. Brittanys are also popular because they combine excellent pointing and retrieving skills. The birds are surprisingly tough for their size, and a good retriever keeps loss of cripples to a minimum.

If birds are running and you're having trouble getting close enough for a shot, try rushing them (below). Or, look for areas that haven't been hunted as hard. By walking a mile or two from the road, you can often find pockets of birds that aren't as spooky.

Once you flush a covey, be sure to mark down singles. They hold extremely tight after the covey breaks up, but they'll start to sneak away unless you get to them in a hurry. Listening for the rallying call, a four-note "chi-ca-go-go," will also help you find singles.

A 20-gauge, 26-inch double-barrel with improved-cylinder and modified chokes is a good choice for Gambel's quail. Most hunters use size 8 field loads, but in the open country, $7\frac{1}{2}$s or 6s will minimize crippling loss. Be sure to wear brush pants and boots with good ankle support. You're most likely to encounter snakes during the early part of the hunting season, but it's possible to run across them anytime, so you should always pack a snakebite kit.

Be sure to carry enough water so you can give your dog a drink every hour or so. Rubber or leather dog boots (below) are recommended because of the cactus, sharp thorns, broken rocks and hot sand. Bring a comb or brush to remove burrs, and forceps or tweezers to pull out cactus spines.

Tips for Hunting Gambel's Quail

OUTFIT your dog with rubber or leather boots to protect its feet from cactus spines. Rubber boots must be taped on; leather boots have laces.

RUSH a flock of Gambel's quail to make them flush, if you see them running. Or, try firing a shot into the air. If you simply walk after them, they'll keep running ahead.

BLOW a quail call to locate the birds; you may get an answer from a nearby covey. A call may also freeze birds that are running.

WORK brushy creek beds by sending one hunter through the densest cover. Unless you have a dog that will penetrate the tangle, this is the only way to flush the birds.

CALIFORNIA QUAIL resemble Gambel's quail because of the black, teardrop-shaped plume, but the buff-colored abdomen has a coarse scale pattern; the back and lower neck, a fine pattern. Both sexes have bluish gray to gray chests and brownish flanks, but males (right) have a black throat, buff-colored forehead and rusty patch behind the plume. Females (left) are similar in appearance, but have a smaller plume and no black throat patch.

California Quail

A favorite among western bird hunters, the California quail is more abundant than the similar-looking Gambel's quail, holds much better for a pointing dog and tends to flush rather than run.

California quail can tolerate a much broader scope of habitat than the Gambel's. They inhabit a 2,000-mile range, extending from southern British Columbia to the tip of the Baja Peninsula. This area includes everything from semidesert, sagebrush habitat to cool, wet coastal forest to scrubby tropical forest.

The birds are most commonly found in open grassy habitat (opposite). They seldom live in uninterrupted forest or brushland. The fact that they inhabit foothills and valleys at elevations of 4,000 feet or less explains why they're often called "valley quail."

California quail form very large coveys, numbering from 20 to 50 birds during the hunting season, and up to 500 birds in winter. When a covey breaks up, the birds utter a three-note rallying call, a distinctive "chi-ca-go."

The abundance of California quail, like that of other western quail, depends mainly on rainfall. Moisture is needed to grow weed seeds and grasses, which are the staples of their diet. They also eat seeds and leaves of alfalfa and clover, as well as cultivated grains, mainly wheat. Most feeding is done early and late in the day.

How you hunt California quail depends on the density of the cover. If possible, avoid hunting them in very sparse vegetation, because they'll probably run rather than fly. If there's no choice but to hunt sparse cover, use the same techniques you would for scaled quail (p. 111).

BIOLOGY AND RANGE

Common Names: valley quail, topknot quail, blue quail
Close Relatives: Gambel's quail, mountain quail, scaled quail
Length: 9 to 11 inches
Weight: 6 to 7 ounces
Clutch Size: 9 to 15
Breeding Habits: monogamous
Eating Quality: excellent; white breast meat similar to that of bobwhite

Prime spots for hunting California quail include brushy cover in creek valleys; around field edges, water holes and blackberry thickets and, in dry years, around guzzlers.

When hunting ridges, remember that the birds tend to run uphill, much like chukar partridge. In this situation, it pays to hunt in pairs, with one hunter uphill and slightly ahead of the other, just as in chukar hunting (p. 61).

It's often difficult to get within shotgun range of a large covey, so you may have to rush it and try to break it up. Mark down the singles, and listen closely for their rallying calls. Singles and smaller coveys will hold much better.

Because of the birds' tendency to hold tight, pointing dogs are a good choice. Favorite breeds include English setters and pointers, Brittanys, German shorthairs and vizslas. But in dense brush, a small, close-working flusher, such as a Boykin spaniel, will burrow in and root out more birds.

The most popular gun for California quail is a light-weight 20-gauge with an improved-cylinder choke. Use field loads with 7½ or 8 shot. Always wear brush pants and boots that provide good ankle support.

PRIME HABITAT for California quail consists of open grassy cover with some taller trees or brush for roosting, and a reliable supply of water or succulent plants.

Tips for Finding and Hunting California Quail

LOOK for California quail near the canyon rim in early morning. In midday, the birds usually fly down the canyon, into cover that may be impenetrable.

HUNT for singles in isolated patches of brush or grass, after you have broken up the covey. Often, the bird will hold extremely tight, and you'll have to kick it out.

WORK patches of brushy cover no more than waist high. The birds are low flyers, so you may not be able to get a shot if they flush in higher cover.

SURROUND a thicket known to hold a covey, and toss in a rock to flush the birds. If you don't block their escape routes, the birds will simply run out the opposite side.

Mountain Quail

Bagging a mountain quail is the ultimate challenge for upland game bird enthusiasts. A look at the dense cover and steep, rugged, mountainous terrain these birds inhabit immediately explains the difficulty of hunting them. In fact, some of the habitat they occupy is considered unhuntable. There are some other problems too: the birds' wary nature and penchant to run instead of fly.

Found in Pacific coastal mountains at altitudes from 2,000 to 10,000 feet, mountain quail are the largest quail species in the United States. They're most commonly associated with *chaparral* (opposite) but are also found along brushy creek corridors, on live-oak hillsides and in new-growth clear-cuts.

In areas with heavy snowfall, the birds may migrate to lower altitudes in winter, but most popula-

---

BIOLOGY AND RANGE

Common Names: mountain partridge, plumed quail

Close Relatives: California quail, scaled quail, Gambel's quail

Length: 10 to 12 inches

Weight: 8 to 10 ounces

Clutch Size: 8 to 12

Breeding Habits: monogamous

Eating Quality: excellent; white breast meat much like that of bobwhite, but breast is larger

MOUNTAIN QUAIL have a tall, straight, black plume made up of two narrow feathers. A white streak separates the chestnut throat from the slate-gray neck. The back and tail are olive-gray to brownish, and the flanks have distinct black-and-white bars. The coloration of males and females is identical.

QUAIL

tions move very little over the course of the year.

Mountain quail thrive on fruits and berries, such as wild grape, service-berry, snowberry, hackberry and manzanito berry. They also eat acorns, grasses, weed seeds, tubers, bulbs and some insects. They require a good supply of water and are usually found near streams or standing pools.

Mountain quail populations, like those of other western quail, undergo major fluctuations, depending mainly on rainfall. Populations are highest when heavy late-winter and early-spring rains produce lush crops of weeds and grasses that young birds need for food. Mountain quail coveys are smaller than those of other quail, generally numbering fewer than ten birds.

The best place to hunt mountain quail is in habitat consisting of no more than 50 percent brushy cover. Heavier cover may be impenetrable for hunters and dogs. Walk the ridges early and late in the day, preferably with a partner walking parallel to you, just as you would for chukars (p. 61).

Because of the bird's larger size and its tendency to flush at longer distances than bobwhites, most hunters use a lightweight 12- or 20-gauge shotgun with a modified choke and high-power loads with 6 or 7½ shot. Be sure to wear brush pants and boots with good ankle support.

Close-working pointers, such as German shorthairs, are the best choice for hunting mountain quail. They'll penetrate the dense cover and pin down coveys, giving you time to climb steep slopes or push your way through heavy brush to get into position for a shot. Short-hairs also do a good job of retrieving birds in the thick tangle.

After flushing a covey, you can sometimes pinpoint singles by listening for the rallying call, a softly whistled "wh-wh-wh-wh-wh-wh."

HABITAT for mountain quail at high altitude (left) consists mainly of brushlands sprinkled with tall conifers. At lower altitude (right), they prefer steep chaparral: brushlands with scrub oaks, thorny bushes and shrubs.

Tips for Hunting Mountain Quail

WATCH for birds running uphill or sneaking away through the rocks and brush. You may have to fire a shot in their direction to make them fly.

WALK down to a covey your dog is pointing, while another hunter posts below it. If you walk up on the birds, they will run uphill rather than flush.

HUNT along steep-sided logging roads, letting your dog work well ahead. Normally, coveys are just downhill or uphill of the road.

CONSERVE energy by sending your dog up or down slopes to find birds. Otherwise, the steep terrain will wear you out in a hurry.

MEARNS QUAIL males have a striking "clown-face" pattern of white patches separated by black streaks. They have a rusty crest, a black breast and undersides, white or cinnamon-colored spots on the flanks, and a grayish brown back and wings. Females (inset) have a buff or cinnamon background coloration with black flecks, and a whitish chin and throat. The back and wings of both sexes have light-colored streaks.

Mearns Quail

Many a Mearns quail hunter has stopped to take a breather, only to be startled by a covey of the birds exploding at his feet. The birds' near-perfect camouflage, combined with their super-tight-holding habits, explains why a good hunting dog is a must.

Although this bird is called Mearns quail throughout its U.S. range, its official name is Montezuma quail, because its native range is mainly in Mexico. Its present range extends northward into Arizona, New Mexico and Texas. Besides Mexico, only Arizona and New Mexico have an open season.

Mearns quail thrive in mountainous country with grassy valleys and rocky ridges sprinkled with junipers and dotted with clusters of live oak (opposite). Typically found at altitudes of 3,500 to 9,000 feet, Mearns quail move very little throughout the year. Like other birds that rely heavily on dense, grassy cover, they cannot tolerate overgrazing.

The birds roost in low grassy areas at night and move up the ridges, feeding in tight family groups of 6 to 12 birds, during the day. They scratch for bulbs

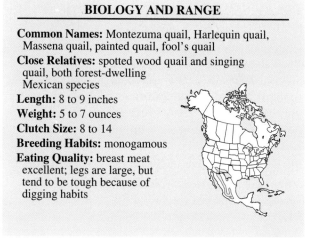

BIOLOGY AND RANGE

Common Names: Montezuma quail, Harlequin quail, Massena quail, painted quail, fool's quail

Close Relatives: spotted wood quail and singing quail, both forest-dwelling Mexican species

Length: 8 to 9 inches

Weight: 5 to 7 ounces

Clutch Size: 8 to 14

Breeding Habits: monogamous

Eating Quality: breast meat excellent; legs are large, but tend to be tough because of digging habits

Tips for Hunting Mearns Quail

LOOK for fresh scratchings made by the birds' big claws (inset) at the bottoms of ravines. The birds roost near the bottom at night and work their way uphill during the day.

HUNT the ridgetops in midday, because most of the birds have scratched their way up the hills by then. They usually feed in coveys, so be alert for a covey flush.

Typical Mearns quail habitat

and tubers, their favorite foods, and also eat acorns, seeds and insects. Hunters commonly locate areas birds are using by looking for their scratchings and chalky white droppings.

Because of their tendency to hold tight, Mearns quail are the ideal bird for pointing dogs. Good choices include English pointers and setters, vizslas and weimaraners. But wide-ranging pointers may be tough to find in the brushy cover. A beeper collar (p. 120) helps you locate your dog when it's on point.

The hot, dry climate and rugged terrain quickly take their toll on even a well-conditioned dog. Carry plenty of water, and don't work the dog too hard. Some hunters bring along several dogs, using one for a few hours at a time, while resting the others.

The usual hunting strategy is to start at the bottom of a ridge and work your way up, because that's the way the birds feed. When they dig for bulbs and tubers, they evidently leave a lot of scent, so a good bird dog can easily track them uphill and pin them down.

A proven two-man technique is for one hunter to walk halfway up the slope, and the other, along the bottom, with the dog working between them. The birds normally flush downhill, so the bottom hunter usually gets the best shots.

When you flush a covey, mark down singles; then thoroughly work the area where they landed. The birds will hold extremely tight and emit very little scent, so they're difficult to find.

In hot weather, work the north slopes, where the soil is moister and birds can scratch more easily. In cool weather, hunt warmer south slopes. Normally, hunting is best from midmorning to late afternoon, after the birds have had a chance to move around and leave a scent trail. But in very hot weather, you'll do better early and late in the day; midday hunting is tough on hunters and dogs, and birds are less active.

There's plenty of thorny brush in Mearns quail country, so hunters should wear brush pants, and dogs, leather boots. Since nearly all shots are close-range, use a 20-gauge shotgun with a skeet, cylinder or improved-cylinder choke, and size 8 field loads.

Scaled Quail

Scaled quail routinely outwit hunters by scurrying ahead and scattering, then holding tight as the hunters walk past them. These highly effective escape tactics led one frustrated hunter to suggest they be renamed "gray ghosts."

These desert quail form coveys that number 10 to 30 birds in fall, with larger coveys becoming more common late in the hunting season. When a covey splits up, the birds utter a distinct "pey-cos" rallying call that can help hunters locate them.

"Scalies" get their name from the dark-tipped feathers on their breast, which create a scaled appearance. They're also called "cottontops," because of the white crest on their crown, or "blues," because of their overall bluish cast.

Found mainly in the desert Southwest at elevations of 3,000 to 5,000 feet, scalies prefer an arid climate. But they must have access to water, such as small streams or cattle tanks, and they'll sometimes fly more than one-half mile to find

BIOLOGY AND RANGE

Common Names: scalie, blue quail, blue, blue racer, cottontop
Close Relatives: mountain quail, California quail, Gambel's quail
Length: 10 to 12 inches
Weight: 6 to 7 ounces
Clutch Size: 8 to 12
Breeding Habits: monogamous
Eating Quality: excellent

SCALED QUAIL have an overall bluish gray coloration. Black-tipped feathers on the breast and, to a lesser degree, on the back and abdomen, give the plumage a scaley look. The sexes are similar in appearance, but the bushy crest is usually buff-colored in females; whitish in males.

QUAIL

it. The size of the fall population is strongly related to the amount of summer rain.

Grassland is a crucial component of scaled quail habitat. It provides overhead cover, as well as weed and grass seeds for food. When grasslands disappear from overgrazing, scaled quail populations dwindle.

Typical scaled quail habitat

Scalies will also take cover under tall plants, such as cactus, mesquite or yucca, and they'll feed on cultivated grains, such as sorghum, wheat and corn.

Although the birds are runners, they'll hold long enough for close shots in dense grassy cover. If you see a covey running ahead of you and there is no cover to hold them, try rushing them. You may not get a shot when they flush, but you can mark down the singles and go after them. Look for a landmark, such as a windmill or tall cactus, to pinpoint their location; then walk right toward it. The singles hold extremely tight, even in grass only an inch or two high.

Often, the covey will refuse to flush. It just runs ahead and breaks up into singles and doubles, which run off to the side of the hunter's path and seemingly disappear. Should this happen, turn around and work back in a zigzag path, checking any patches of grass or tall plants that may conceal the birds.

Many scalie hunters use big-running pointers to locate coveys in the open grasslands. They may flush some coveys too far ahead, but then you can hunt for singles, which are much easier for the dog to pin down. The dog may also pin down singles that scurry off to the side as the covey runs ahead. Some hunters prefer closer-working pointers that won't push the coveys as far.

Even though scalies usually flush at long distances, it's best to use a 12- to 20-gauge shotgun with a choke no tighter than improved-cylinder, because of the excellent close-range shooting for singles. Use field loads with 7½ or 8 shot.

Tips for Finding and Hunting Scaled Quail

FIND a water hole you know the birds are using; then walk around it in ever-increasing circles. Seldom will they go more than one-half mile from their water source.

LOOK for scalies around man-made cover, such as tractors and other old farm equipment. Brush piles also make good scalie cover.

PRACTICE shooting at low-flying clay targets, which mimic the flight pattern of scaled quail. Because the birds often take off from a dead run, they fly at a low angle.

CARRY a plastic squirt bottle for watering your dog while afield. This way, the dog won't overheat before it can get back to the car for a drink.

Migratory Upland Game Birds

MOURNING DOVES have a slate gray or gray-brown back; a fawn-colored breast and neck, with an iridescent pinkish or greenish cast; and black spots on the wings and neck. The outer tail feathers have grayish white margins. The sexes are similar in appearance, but females are slightly smaller than males.

Mourning Doves

The mourning dove's twisting, darting, speedy flight makes it one of the favorites of upland bird hunters – and *the* favorite of ammunition manufacturers. It takes an average of 8 shots to drop a dove, and hunters bag nearly 50 million of them a year.

Despite this tremendous harvest, the continental mourning dove population is about 500 million, making it the most numerous North American game bird. It is also the most widely distributed, occurring in every state, every Canadian province bordering the U.S., and all of Mexico.

Most everyone is familiar with the male dove's mating call, the mournful five- to seven-note cooing sound heard in spring. After mating, the female lays two eggs in a poorly constructed nest made of sticks loosely placed in shrubs, bushes, crotches of trees, on the ground or even on a windowsill. She may also use the nest of another bird. Doves are masters at the "broken-wing act," feigning injury to lure intruders away from the nest.

The dove's ability to nest in such a variety of habitat types and raise multiple broods, sometimes four or more per year, explains why populations remain high and relatively stable. Even under conditions that raise havoc with most other game bird populations, such as bad weather or high predator counts, at least one brood is likely to survive.

Though considered an upland game bird for hunting purposes, the mourning dove is actually a migratory bird. They nest and spend their summer as far north as southern Canada. But they will not tolerate cold weather, and the first below-freezing nights in fall send them winging southward. Migrating flocks usually number fewer than a dozen birds, but may include more than 100. They winter as far south as Panama. Some, however, spend their entire life in a warm climate and do not migrate.

Adult doves feed heavily on seeds, such as those of doveweed, foxtail, ragweed and wild hemp. But in fall, they flock to harvested crop fields to feed on corn, soybeans, oats, wheat and sunflower seeds.

The birds feed early and late in the day, usually in idle crop fields or other open fields. They prefer to pick up seeds on open ground and will not feed in dense grassy or brushy cover.

After feeding, they pick up grit along gravel roads and fly to water. Then, they fly to their roosting areas, usually dead trees within two miles of their watering sites. They normally use the same watering and roosting areas at night as they did in midday.

Doves normally fly in a fairly straight line, at speeds of 30 to 40 miles per hour. But they're capable of highly erratic flight at speeds up to 55 when they're trying to evade avian predators – and hunters.

Hunting for doves is currently banned in 13 states, mostly in the North. Wildlife managers in most of these states favor a dove season, but have not been able to sell the idea to the public. Preservationists maintain that the dove is "the bird of peace" and should not be legal quarry for hunters. Ironically, many of the birds saved in the North are later killed in the South or in Mexico.

BIOLOGY AND RANGE

Common Names: turtle dove, dove

Close Relatives: domestic pigeon, band-tailed pigeon, white-winged dove

Length: 11 to 13 inches

Weight: 3½ to 5 ounces

Clutch Size: 2 per clutch; several clutches per year

Breeding Habits: monogamous

Eating Quality: very good; breast is small with dark meat

YOUNG DOVES are nurtured on *crop milk,* a high-protein, milklike substance shed from the crop walls. This special diet contributes to their high survival rate.

Water holes with muddy, gradually sloping shorelines are prime dove-hunting areas

Techniques for Hunting Mourning Doves

In the North, the best time to hunt doves is in early season, when local birds are still around and haven't grown wary of hunters. Southern hunters enjoy steady action throughout the season, but the pace picks up shortly after cold, stormy weather in the North drives large numbers of doves southward.

Perfect dove-hunting weather is a warm, calm day after the birds have moved in. They'll stay around as long as the weather is warm and stable. Doves seldom fly in rainy weather.

A good retriever is recommended for all types of dove hunting. With this many birds coming in, there are bound to be some cripples.

Dove hunters employ a wide variety of hunting strategies, most involving pass-shooting birds flying into feeding or watering sites.

Pass-shooting near feeding fields is the most widely used method. Once they zero in on a field, they'll continue to use it unless they're driven away by heavy hunting pressure. A recently harvested field, however, may draw birds away from other feeding fields.

Before selecting a pass-shooting spot, watch carefully to see where the birds are flying. They may consistently fly through a certain gap in the trees or skirt the end of a treeline projecting into a feeding field. When you identify the most promising flight path, look for a brush clump or some other kind of cover that will break your silhouette. Wear camouflage or drab brown clothing for all types of dove hunting.

When hunting alone, look for a small field; this way, the birds will be in range when they fly by. It takes

Tips for Hunting Doves

PLACE dove decoys in trees or on fencelines adjacent to feeding fields or water holes, or in funnels between feeding, watering or roosting areas.

PASS-SHOOT doves as they fly into feeding fields. To determine where the birds are feeding, spend some time scouting before the season opens.

SET UP a camouflage ground blind if the cover is not sufficient to hide a standing hunter.

LOOK for doves roosting on power lines or in dead trees prior to or during the hunting season. If you see plenty of birds, hunt surrounding fields.

KEEP your doves cool by placing them in a small cooler, which can double as a shooting seat.

several hunters to cover a large field and keep the birds flying. For safety purposes, take careful note of where all hunters are positioned, and do not shoot at low-flying birds.

The ideal gun for pass-shooting doves is a 12-gauge pump or semi-automatic with a modified choke and 28- to 30-inch barrel, with size 7½ or 8 field loads.

If nobody else is hunting a feeding field, you can jump-shoot birds that get by you and land, assuming there is enough cover to conceal your approach. You can also jump-shoot doves in their midday roosting areas.

Because mourning doves usually fly to water after feeding, it pays to do some scouting to find their watering sites. The best water holes have a bare, gradually sloping shoreline, so the birds can easily walk into the water, and enough trees, brush or tall grass to conceal the hunters.

You can simply pass-shoot the birds as they fly into water holes, or set decoys (above) to draw the birds into shotgun range. Because this type of hunting offers fast action and close-range shooting, the best shotgun is a 20-gauge semi-automatic or pump with a 26-inch barrel and improved-cylinder choke, with size 8 field loads.

Pass-shooting along flight paths between feeding, watering or roosting sites is a good strategy when fields and water holes are being hunted heavily. Look for natural funnels, such as a cut in the trees, between these areas. The narrower the funnel, the better; this way, the birds are more likely to fly within shooting range. Placing a few decoys in lone dead trees or on fences will also pull in some birds. If you can't find tall cover for concealment, look for a shady spot where you'll be less visible, or set up a blind (above). Use the same guns and ammo as you would for hunting near feeding fields.

Woodcock

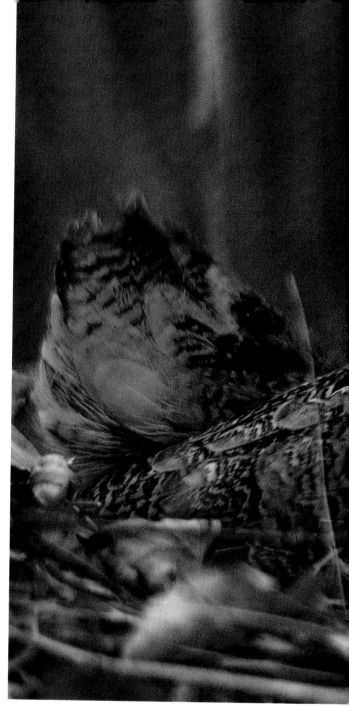

WOODCOCK have brown, black and rust-colored mottling on the back and sides; black bars on top of the head

If the ground is full of boreholes and covered with "chalk," you're in woodcock country. Woodcock use their long bill to probe for earthworms and grubs, their favorite foods, leaving distinct round holes.

Woodcock do most of their feeding around dawn and dusk, usually in open areas with dark, moist soil. Besides worms and grubs, they eat insects, weed seeds, berries and green leaves. During midday, they retreat to brushy cover. On hot days, you'll find them beneath evergreens or in other shady spots. When the weather is cool, they're more likely to be on a sunny hillside or in a sunlit opening in the woods.

Although woodcock are officially classified as migratory shorebirds, they're commonly found in much the same kind of habitat as ruffed grouse and are usually considered to be upland game birds in hunting literature.

Male woodcock are known for their elaborate breeding display. In spring, they establish *singing grounds*, open areas in or adjacent to a young forest or wetland, in the northern part of their range. Around dusk, a male begins *peenting*, making a "bzzt, bzzt, bzzt" sound while walking around and bobbing his head. He then flies straight upward in narrowing circles, with wings whistling, to an altitude of about 200 feet. Then he spirals back down, uttering a musical "chickaree, chickaree." He repeats this display until he attracts a female. The birds, which live as long as 5 years, return to the same areas to breed each spring.

A female lays four eggs in a shallow, leaf-lined depression in a brushy area near the singing ground. While incubating the eggs, she remains perfectly motionless and relies on her near-perfect camouflage to fool predators.

The eggs hatch in 20 days, and the young mature rapidly. By the age of 2 months, they've separated from the parents and are feeding on their own.

Alder thickets, especially those within an aspen forest, make prime woodcock habitat. The thickets usually block out enough sunlight that the ground beneath them stays bare, so woodcock have no trouble probing for worms. You'll also find birds around low-lying willow and birch thickets, along stream courses, around edges of marshes and in clear-cuts, especially those from 5 to 10 years old.

After a hard frost, woodcock have difficulty probing for worms, so they fly south on the first strong northerly wind. They begin migrating in early to mid-October, usually following major north-south river valleys. Because they fly at night, they're seldom seen migrating. They migrate in loose groups, and remain loosely grouped after they arrive at their

and eyes set toward the rear of the head. The sexes look similar, but females are noticeably larger than males with a slightly longer bill. An adult female's bill measures more than 2¾ inches; a male's, less than 2½.

destination. Woodcock winter in the south-central and southeastern states.

In a normal year, when there has been adequate rain-fall in late summer, woodcock trickle through for a month or so. But if the ground is very dry or freezes early, they may pour through in a few days, greatly shortening the hunting season.

The woodcock's tight-holding habits make it ideal quarry for pointing-dog enthusiasts. Add to this the bird's erratic, evasive in-flight maneuvering, and it's easy to understand why so many wingshots hold the woodcock in high esteem.

BIOLOGY AND RANGE

Common Names: timberdoodle, woody, wood snipe, bec, bog sucker

Close Relatives: sandpipers, snipe

Length: male - 10 to 11 inches
             female - 11 to 12 inches

Weight: male - 4½ to 7 ounces
             female - 6 to 9 ounces

Clutch Size: 4

Breeding Habits: polygamous

Eating Quality: dark breast meat, which many say has a liver taste

OUTFIT your pointer with a beeper collar when hunting in thick cover. This way, you will know when the dog goes on point, because the interval between beeps or the tone of the beeps will change.

Techniques for Hunting Woodcock

To be a successful woodcock hunter, you must become familiar with their migration patterns and learn to identify their preferred habitat.

Because woodcock do not migrate until the first hard frost, hunting is usually better in midseason than it was earlier. Early-season hunters in the northern part of the range may find good numbers of local birds, but the thick foliage makes hunting tough. And by late season, the birds are usually gone.

Experienced woodcock hunters prefer below-freezing nighttime temperatures and strong northerly winds. Weather dictates how long migrating woodcock remain in a given area. They do not like fighting a headwind, so they stay around longest when winds are from the south.

A single hunter with a good dog can easily work typical woodcock cover. Most hunters prefer close-to mid-ranging pointers, such as Brittanys and English setters. Woodcock may run a bit, but they seldom go far. The dog will pin down the bird, usually in a clump of grass or brush, and you'll have plenty of time to get into position for a shot. When a woodcock flushes, it normally heads for an opening in the surrounding trees or brush. Try to anticipate its flight path, and position yourself accordingly for the best shot.

When your dog goes on point, you may have trouble spotting it in the dense cover. Some woodcock hunters use bells or electronic beeper collars (left) to keep track of their dogs. A white dog is much easier to see than a dark one.

If you don't have a dog, try the walk-and-wait technique. You may have to pause near a likely clump of cover for 30 seconds or more to make the bird nervous enough to flush. Should you miss the bird, keep your eye on it; seldom will it fly more than 100 yards.

Although woodcock are challenging targets, you can boost your odds of hitting them by taking your time. The bird rises rapidly on the initial flush, so the tendency is to shoot under it. If you wait until it levels off, you're much more likely to connect.

Banding a woodcock chick

Pointing-dog enthusiasts are finding that springtime woodcock banding, done under permit in some states, is a good way to get in extra dog work, while contributing to movement studies. When the dog points a hen and chicks on a nest, you catch them with a big net, band them, measure the chicks' bills to determine their age and release them.

Recommended gear for woodcock hunting includes waterproof boots and brush pants. If the ground is extra moist, you may need rubber boots. Be sure to wear some blaze orange so you're easily visible in the heavy cover.

A 20- or 28-gauge double-barrel with cylinder and improved-cylinder chokes makes the perfect woodcock gun. Repeaters are not necessary for woodcock hunting, because you rarely get more than two shots at a bird, and multiple flushes are rare. Besides, true woodcock devotees consider repeaters unethical. Most hunters prefer size 8 field loads, but if there are ruffed grouse in the area as well, 7½s are a better choice.

PRIME HABITAT for woodcock has moist ground with very little ground foliage but dense above-ground cover. This way, the birds are protected from predators, yet they can easily probe for worms in the exposed soil.

Tips for Hunting Woodcock

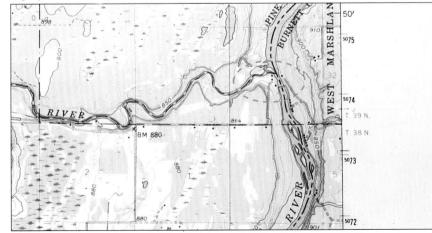

IDENTIFY woodcock migration routes by referring to a U.S. Geological Survey Quad Map. Look for spots where major north-south river valleys intersect with east-west tributaries. When the wind is from the south, you'll find woodcock along the lower ends of these tributaries.

LOOK for chalk marks or "whitewash." It's easily washed away by precipitation, so finding some usually means woodcock are nearby.

Other Migratory Upland Game Birds

BAND-TAILED PIGEON. Hunted mainly in California, Oregon and Washington, these birds are strongly linked to pine-oak forests.

Good-sized birds measuring about 14 inches long and weighing 9 to 12 ounces, bandtails are bluish gray with a dark gray band across the tail (inset) and a white band across the back of the neck.

COMMON SNIPE. Sometimes called Wilson's snipe or jack snipe, this widely distributed game bird is found in marshes and wet meadows from Alaska through Central America.

Often confused with the woodcock, the snipe prefers somewhat wetter ground. It has a similar long bill, used to probe for worms and grubs, but is much smaller, weighing only about 4 ounces.

WHITE-WINGED DOVE.
Although whitewings are hunted most heavily in northeastern Mexico, some are taken in Texas and Arizona. Huge whitewing flocks congregate in grain fields before the early-fall migration.

Slightly larger than a mourning dove, the whitewing has a distinct white band along the edge of the wing.

WHITE-TIPPED DOVE. Unlike other doves, whitetips are not truly migratory. They range from Mexico into southern Texas, the only place in the United States where it is legal to hunt them. Look for them in brushy thickets and citrus groves.

About the size of mourning doves, whitetips have a grayish body and the tail has white outer feathers near the tip; the undersides of the wings are rust-colored.

INDEX

Cy DeCosse Incorporated offers a variety of how-to books. For information write:
  Cy DeCosse Subscriber Books
  5900 Green Oak Drive
  Minnetonka, MN 55343

Photo Credits

Cooperating Guides

Rodger Affeldt
Rodger's Guide Service
Garrison, North Dakota 58540
(701) 337-5572
Pheasant

Larry Brooks
Dakota Outfitters Unlimited
829 East View Drive
Bismarck, North Dakota 58501
(701) 224-0494
Pheasant, Sharp-tailed Grouse, Hungarian Partridge

Jeff Crosland
Crooked River Kennels
14232 South 131st Street
Gilbert, Arizona 85234
(602) 821-9408
Gambel's Quail, Scaled Quail

Curt Granthen, Carey Powell
Dos Cabezas Guide Service
2928 North 35th Avenue #5
Phoenix, Arizona 85017
(602) 447-0786
Gambel's Quail, Scaled Quail

Steve Grossman
Little Moran Hunting Club
Route 1 - Staples, Minnesota 56479
(218) 894-3852
Ruffed and Sharp-tailed Grouse, Woodcock, Pheasant

Pat Holbrook
Top Notch Guide Service
1434 Johnson Street
Red Bluff, California 96080
(916) 527-5686
Mountain Quail, California Quail

Byron and Tolly Holtan
Indian Hills Resort
Box 700 - Garrison, North Dakota 58540
(701) 743-4122
Pheasant, Sharp-tailed Grouse, Hungarian Partridge, Mourning Dove

Shannon Lindsay
River Mountain Ranch
Box 16 - White Bird, Idaho 83554
(208) 838-2273
Chukar and Hungarian Partridge, California Quail, Blue Grouse, Ruffed Grouse

Dan and Dean Priest
Box 37982 - Phoenix, Arizona 85069
(602) 867-1056
Mearns, Gambel's and Scaled Quail

Mike Smyth
Cimarron River Guided Hunts
Box 656 - Ashland, Kansas 67831
(316) 635-2261
Prairie Chicken, Bobwhite Quail

Dan Torrence
Walnut Valley Guide Service
Box 838 - Winfield, Kansas 67156
(316) 221-3767
Prairie Chicken, Bobwhite Quail